McDougal Littell
LITERATURE

GRAMMAR FOR WRITING
Workbook
Grade 6

McDougal Littell
EVANSTON, ILLINOIS • BOSTON • DALLAS

Warning: Permission is hereby granted to teachers to reprint or photocopy in classroom quantities the pages or sheets in this work that carry the following copyright notice: Copyright © McDougal Littell/Houghton Mifflin Company. These pages are designed to be reproduced by teachers for use in their classes with accompanying McDougal Littell material, provided each copy made shows the copyright notice. Such copies may not be sold, and further distribution is expressly prohibited. Except as authorized above, prior written permission must be obtained from McDougal Littell to reproduce or transmit this work or portions thereof in any other form or by any electronic or mechanical means, including any information storage or retrieval system, unless expressly permitted by federal copyright law. Address inquiries to Supervisor, Rights and Permissions, McDougal Littell, P.O. Box 1667, Evanston, IL 60204. Manufactured in the U.S.A.

ISBN-10: 0-618-90644-4
ISBN-13: 978-0-618-90644-4

Copyright © McDougal Littell, a division of Houghton Mifflin Company. All rights reserved.

19 20 0928 16 15

4500535003

Contents

Copyright © McDougal Littell/Houghton Mifflin Company.

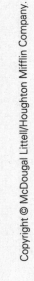

Copyright © McDougal Littell/Houghton Mifflin Company.

Special Features

The *Grammar, Usage, and Mechanics Copymasters/ Workbook* contains a wealth of skill-building exercises.

Each lesson has different levels of worksheets. **Teaching** introduces the skill; **More Practice** and **Application** extend the skill with advanced exercises.

Name _____ Date _____

Lesson 1

Complete Subjects and Predicates

Teaching

A **sentence** is a group of words that expresses a complete thought. Every complete sentence has two basic parts: a subject and a predicate.

The **complete subject** includes all the words that tell whom or what the sentence is about.

<u>Nine planets</u> orbit the sun.

The **complete predicate** includes the verb and all the words that tell what the subject is or what the subject does.

The word *planet* <u>comes from a Greek word meaning "wanderer."</u>

Identifying Complete Subjects and Complete Predicates

Underline the complete subject once and the complete predicate twice.

   EXAMPLE <u>Light from the sun</u> <u>makes life possible on Earth</u>.

1. The sun is much bigger than all the other planets.
2. Planets in the solar system reflect light from the sun.
3. Stars twinkle in the sky at night.
4. Planets shine with a steadier light.
5. Stars such as our sun make their own light and heat.
6. Some of the planets have satellites, or moons.
7. Our planet has only one satellite.
8. The largest planet is Jupiter.
9. Asteroids, meteoroids, and comets belong to our solar system.
10. Many of the asteroids orbit in an area between Mars and Jupiter.
11. The surface of Mercury is covered with many craters.
12. Masses of clouds cover the surface of Venus.
13. Large amounts of iron in its rocks give Mars a reddish color.
14. One of the moons of Jupiter is named *Ganymede*.
15. Ganymede is the biggest satellite in our solar system.
16. The rings of Saturn can be seen through a telescope.
17. The *Voyager 2* mission discovered ten new moons of Uranus.
18. *Voyager* sent scientists new information about Neptune.
19. Many astronomers use telescopes for studying the universe.
20. Some astronomers analyze light and radio waves.
21. The Hubble Space Telescope sends scientists new information daily.
22. The planets closest to Earth are Mercury, Venus, and Mars.

Each page focuses on one topic or skill. A brief instructional summary on the **Teaching** page is followed by reinforcement activities.

Key words and phrases are highlighted for greater clarity and ease of use.

When appropriate, example sentences demonstrate how to complete exercises.

Tabs make it easy to navigate the book.

CHAPTER 1

Copyright © McDougal Littell/Houghton Mifflin Company.

Copyright © McDougal Littell Inc.

1

Name _____ Date _____

Lesson 1

Complete Subjects and Predicates

Teaching

A **sentence** is a group of words that expresses a complete thought. Every complete sentence has two basic parts: a subject and a predicate.

The **complete subject** includes all the words that tell whom or what the sentence is about.

> <u>Nine planets</u> orbit the sun.

The **complete predicate** includes the verb and all the words that tell what the subject is or what the subject does.

> The word *planet* <u>comes from a Greek word meaning "wanderer."</u>

Identifying Complete Subjects and Complete Predicates

Underline the complete subject once and the complete predicate twice.

EXAMPLE <u>Light from the sun</u> <u>makes life possible on Earth</u>.

1. The sun is much bigger than all the other planets.
2. Planets in the solar system reflect light from the sun.
3. Stars twinkle in the sky at night.
4. Planets shine with a steadier light.
5. Stars such as our sun make their own light and heat.
6. Some of the planets have satellites, or moons.
7. Our planet has only one satellite.
8. The largest planet is Jupiter.
9. Asteroids, meteoroids, and comets belong to our solar system.
10. Many of the asteroids orbit in an area between Mars and Jupiter.
11. The surface of Mercury is covered with many craters.
12. Masses of clouds cover the surface of Venus.
13. Large amounts of iron in its rocks give Mars a reddish color.
14. One of the moons of Jupiter is named *Ganymede.*
15. Ganymede is the biggest satellite in our solar system.
16. The rings of Saturn can be seen through a telescope.
17. The *Voyager 2* mission discovered ten new moons of Uranus.
18. *Voyager* sent scientists new information about Neptune.
19. Many astronomers use telescopes for studying the universe.
20. Some astronomers analyze light and radio waves.
21. The Hubble Space Telescope sends scientists new information daily.
22. The planets closest to Earth are Mercury, Venus, and Mars.

Copyright © McDougal Littell/Houghton Mifflin Company.

Lesson 1

Complete Subjects and Predicates

More Practice

CHAPTER 1

A. Identifying Complete Subjects and Predicates

Draw a vertical line between the complete subject and the complete predicate in each of the following sentences.

EXAMPLE Stony meteors | are found in outer space.

1. Meteors sometimes enter Earth's atmosphere.
2. Friction with the air makes the meteors glow.
3. Glowing meteors are called falling stars.
4. Some fast meteors travel about 26 miles per second.
5. Large swarms of meteors enter Earth's atmosphere several times each year.
6. The shower of sparks from the meteors appears in the sky.
7. People throughout Earth's history have seen meteor showers.
8. A meteorite is a meteor that reaches the surface of Earth.
9. Some meteorites cause huge craters in Earth's surface.
10. The largest meteorite now on Earth weighs about 66 tons.

B. Using Complete Subjects and Predicates

On the line to the right of each item, write how each group of words could be used: **CS** for a complete subject or **CP** for a complete predicate. Then use each group of words in a complete sentence, adding a complete subject or complete predicate as needed.

EXAMPLE a high bridge *CS*
          A high bridge crossed the river.

1. set the table for dinner   _____

_____

2. a newborn kitten   _____

_____

3. ghost stories   _____

_____

4. broke the school record   _____

_____

5. gave her friend a gift   _____

_____

Copyright © McDougal Littell/Houghton Mifflin Company.

Lesson 1

Complete Subjects and Predicates

Application

A. Revising by Adding Details

Add details to the subjects and predicates to make more interesting sentences.

1. Planets move.

_____

2. Stars twinkle.

_____

3. Spaceships travel.

_____

4. Astronauts train.

_____

5. Satellites circle.

_____

6. The universe expands.

_____

B. Writing with Complete Subjects and Complete Predicates

Imagine that you have taken these notes for a report. As you review your notes, rewrite fragments as complete sentences. Each sentence must have a complete subject and predicate. You may combine two or more fragments in a single sentence.

Asteroids. Made of dark, rocky matter. Have different sizes and shapes. Revolve around the sun. Mainly between orbits of Mars and Jupiter. Thousands·known to astronomers. Ceres the largest and discovered first, January 1, 1801. Others—Pallas, Juno, Vesta. Sometimes collide with each other. Pieces that fall to Earth called meteorites. New ones still being discovered.

_____

_____

_____

_____

_____

_____

_____

_____

Copyright © McDougal Littell/Houghton Mifflin Company.

CHAPTER 1

Simple Subjects

Teaching

The **simple subject** is the main word or words in the complete subject. Words that describe the subject are not part of the simple subject. In the following sentences, the simple subjects are underlined.

<u>Insects</u> all over the world are fascinating.
COMPLETE SUBJECT   COMPLETE PREDICATE

If a proper name is used as the subject, all parts of the name make up the simple subject.

<u>Professor Miller</u> at the university studies insects.
COMPLETE SUBJECT   COMPLETE PREDICATE

Identifying Simple Subjects

Underline the simple subject in each sentence.

1. Large dragonflies dart around the pond.
2. Honeybees gather nectar in the flowers.
3. The chocolate chip cookie was covered with ants.
4. Wasps often build their nests underground.
5. Monarch butterflies travel to warmer places when the weather gets too cold.
6. My brother likes to catch fireflies at night.
7. Grandmother's woolen scarf had a moth hole in it.
8. Some large insects measure four inches in length.
9. Mosquito bites are very itchy.
10. Dr. Davis at the animal clinic treated my dog for fleas.
11. More insects live on Earth than any other living creature.
12. Beetles that live in the ground are hard to see.
13. The katydid looks like a leaf on a tree.
14. Certain insects have learned to live in hot springs or in freezing water.
15. Kindly Mrs. Danforth helped remove the stinger from my arm.
16. The silk for this blouse was produced by silkworms.
17. A green caterpillar was eating the cabbage in the garden.
18. Governor Jones surveyed the crops damaged by the grasshoppers.
19. The beekeeper gathered the honeycombs from her hives.
20. True insects have three body parts and six legs.

Copyright © McDougal Littell/Houghton Mifflin Company.

Lesson 2 Simple Subjects

More Practice

CHAPTER 1

A. Identifying Simple Subjects

Underline the simple subject in each of the following sentences.

1. The dragonfly has different regional names.
2. Dr. Martin at the research center studies malaria, a disease carried by mosquitoes.
3. One boy in our science class collects butterflies.
4. Gypsy moth caterpillars damaged hundreds of trees in the park.
5. Locusts travel in huge swarms from one place to another.
6. Wasp stings can be very painful.
7. Mr. Lewis at the agricultural center studies insects and their effect on crops.
8. Some insects are quite colorful.
9. Plant-loving aphids are the favorite food of ladybugs.
10. Pollen is carried from one plant to another by bees and other insects.

B. Writing Simple Subjects

Choose one of the following words to complete each sentence below. Write the simple subject on the line. Cross out each word as you use it.

| spider | wings | caterpillar | moth | eyes |
| ant | honeybees | termites | butterfly | centipede |

1. A _____ spins webs and has eight legs.
2. Two huge _____ help the insect see.
3. _____ fly in and out of their hive all day.
4. A _____ is a long, thin insect with many pairs of legs.
5. Two or four _____ carry some insects from place to place.
6. The _____ is the early stage in the life of a moth or butterfly.
7. Many _____ can damage a home or building by tunneling through the wood.
8. The _____ is an insect whose larvae eat woolen fabric.
9. An _____ can carry objects much heavier than itself.
10. A _____ usually has large colorful wings.

Copyright © McDougal Littell/Houghton Mifflin Company.

CHAPTER 1

Lesson 2

Simple Subjects

Application

A. Writing Simple Subjects in Sentences

Use each of these words as the simple subject in a sentence.

1. bees _____

_____

2. grasshopper _____

_____

3. tarantula_____

_____

4. ladybug _____

_____

5. firefly _____

_____

B. Revising

Read this paragraph carefully. In some sentences, the writer has left out some of
the simple subjects. When you find a sentence without a simple subject, insert this
proofreading symbol ⌃ and write a simple subject in the space above it.

EXAMPLE Some ⌃*insects* are helpful to us.

Insects can be harmful, but they benefit us too. Of course, make honey

that we use for baking and eating. Did you know that silkworms spin silk,

which we make into clothing? Many insects carry pollen to fruit and vegetable

crops. And such as oranges and apples could not produce seeds without

pollination from bees. Some such as peas, onions, and cabbages, would not

grow without the help of insects. In addition, are food for birds, fish, lizards,

and many other animals. Insects are food for certain plants too. Some good,

such as the ladybug, eat other insects that damage plants. In light of how

important insects are to other living things, should realize that insects have

a special role in the balance of nature.

Copyright © McDougal Littell/Houghton Mifflin Company.

Lesson 3

Simple Predicates, or Verbs

Teaching

The **simple predicate,** or **verb** is the main word or words in the complete predicate.

Children around the world <u>love</u> folktales. (*love folktales* is the complete predicate)

VERB

Folktales <u>have been told</u> for centuries.

VERB PHRASE

Verbs are words used to express an action, a condition, or a state of being. **Linking verbs** tell what the subject *is*. **Action verbs** tell what the subject *does,* even when the action cannot be seen.

A folktale <u>is</u> an oral legend or story. (linking)

Many parents <u>tell</u> their children folktales. (action)

Identifying Simple Predicates, or Verbs

Underline the simple predicate, or verb, in each sentence.

1. Folktales are make-believe stories about people and animals.
2. Many English folktales start with the words, "Once upon a time."
3. A version of the Cinderella story exists in many different countries.
4. Many folktales have a handsome prince as the hero.
5. The prince fights many battles against dragons or monsters.
6. Most tales include a beautiful princess.
7. Sometimes, a wicked witch puts the princess under a spell.
8. The courageous prince breaks the evil spell.
9. Other folktales relate stories about animals.
10. The animals act in human ways.
11. In one story, a sly fox fools a crow.
12. Another story tells of a race between a tortoise and a hare.
13. The overconfident hare takes a nap during the race.
14. The slow-moving tortoise wins the race.
15. Often, animals play tricks in these stories.
16. The coyote is the trickster in most American Indian stories.
17. In African stories, a spider tricks other animals.
18. These stories teach lessons to their readers.
19. A story about ants and grasshoppers compares hard workers to lazy ones.
20. People of all ages enjoy folktales.

Copyright © McDougal Littell/Houghton Mifflin Company.

Name _____ Date _____

Lesson 3

Simple Predicates, or Verbs

More Practice

A. Identifying Simple Predicates, or Verbs

Underline the simple predicate, or verb, in each of the following sentences.

1. Legends are a popular kind of folktale.
2. Many stories relate the adventures of Paul Bunyan.
3. Paul was a giant lumberjack from the northern part of America.
4. Babe, a blue ox, helped Paul in the forest.
5. Another legend tells about John Henry.
6. John Henry digs tunnels for the railroad.
7. One time he competes against a steam drill.
8. With only his hammer, John Henry finishes the tunnel first.
9. Pecos Bill invented all the cowboy skills in the West.
10. Once he rode a cyclone instead of his horse.

B. Writing Simple Predicates, or Verbs

Choose one of the following words to complete each sentence below. Write the simple predicate, or verb, on the line. Cross out each verb as you use it.

tell	sees	ride	appears	make
commands	rub	wishes	uses	surprise

1. Some legends _____ the characters larger than life.

2. Captain Stormalong _____ a huge wooden ship.

3. Sailors _____ horses on the gigantic deck of Captain Stormalong's ship.

4. The crew members _____ soap on the sides of the ship to squeeze through the English Channel.

5. Febold Feboldson _____ in stories about the Great Plains.

6. Some tales _____ how Feboldson planted all the cottonwood trees.

7. Feboldson _____ a happy auger to dig hundreds of holes.

8. Paul Bunyan _____ for a giant pancake.

9. His cooks _____ him with a griddle as big as a skating rink.

10. Paul _____ his cooks skating on sticks of butter to grease the griddle.

Copyright © McDougal Littell/Houghton Mifflin Company.

Lesson 3 **Simple Predicates, or Verbs**   *Application*

A. Writing Simple Predicates, or Verbs, in Sentences

Use each of these words as the simple predicate, or verb, in a sentence.

1. find _____

_____

2. enjoy _____

_____

3. forgot _____

_____

4. wished _____

_____

5. laughed _____

_____

6. discovered _____

_____

B. Revising

Read this paragraph carefully. In some sentences, the writer has left out the simple predicates, or verbs. When you find a sentence without a simple predicate, or verb, insert this proofreading symbol ⌃ and write a verb in the space above it to complete the sentence.

                is

EXAMPLE Sir Launfal⌃a British knight.

     The legend of King Arthur and his knights of the Round Table very old. In the story, King Arthur of England is a brave ruler. Many knights serve him. They in battles for the kingdom. They rescue people in need of help. One of these knights Sir Launfal. He dreams of finding the Holy Grail. He for it for many years. Sir Launfal never the Holy Grail. He does have many interesting adventures, however. One day he helps a starving leper. The leper teaches Sir Launfal the meaning of the Holy Grail. He Sir Launfal that the Grail is the symbol of charity and mercy.

Copyright © McDougal Littell/Houghton Mifflin Company.

CHAPTER 1

Copyright © McDougal Littell/Houghton Mifflin Company.

Lesson 4

Verb Phrases

Teaching

The simple predicate, or verb, may consist of two or more words. These words are called the **verb phrase.** A verb phrase is made up of a main verb and one or more helping verbs.

A **main verb** can stand by itself as the simple predicate of a sentence.

> Many different people <u>lived</u> in the American colonies.
> **MAIN VERB** (action)

> The colonists <u>were</u> hardworking.
> **MAIN VERB** (linking)

Helping verbs help the main verb express action or show time.

> Ships from England <u>would bring</u> supplies to the settlers.
> **VERB PHRASE** (*Would* is the helping verb.)

Common Helping Verbs	
Forms of *be*	is, am, was, are, were, be, been
Forms of *do*	do, does, did
Forms of *have*	has, have, had
Others	may, might, can, should, could, would, shall, will

Identifying Verb Phrases

Underline the verb phrase in each sentence. Include main verbs and helping verbs.

1. The colonists would build a home as quickly as possible.
2. Wood from nearby forests was used for their homes.
3. In later years, some houses were made of brick.
4. Poor settlers could make their furniture from the many trees of the forest.
5. Wealthy families could order fancy furniture from England.
6. The colonists may have brought some tools and household items with them.
7. They did eat some new foods, such as corn.
8. Most colonists would wear rough, homemade clothing called homespun.
9. Adults and children did like games and contests.
10. Sometimes, they might fly a kite.
11. Colonial children might have become good at familiar games such as marbles and hopscotch.
12. You would have recognized some of their favorite playthings—jump ropes, dolls, and other toys.
13. Many families would have been the proud owners of pet cats and dogs.
14. Farm children might have owned a pet lamb or pony.
15. Life in colonial times could be both difficult and fun.

Lesson 4 Verb Phrases

More Practice

A. Identifying Main Verbs and Helping Verbs

Underline the main verb once and the helping verb twice in each of the following sentences.

EXAMPLE I <u>am</u> <u>learning</u> about life in colonial America.

1. Master craftsmen would teach young boys certain skills.
2. The young boys were called apprentices.
3. Some apprentices could learn all about fine furniture.
4. Others might be taught about the printing press.
5. An especially talented boy would be apprenticed to a lawyer or doctor.
6. Some girls were trained as housekeepers or cooks.
7. Many children did attend some type of school.
8. All should have learned daily living skills from their parents.
9. A farm boy would help his father with the chores.
10. A girl's mother would show her daughter how to spin and weave.

B. Writing Verb Phrases

Add a helping verb to complete the verb phrase in each sentence below.

1. Some families _____ visit colonial towns such as Williamsburg, Virginia.

2. _____ you toured the Governor's Palace there?

3. A visitor _____ see how people in the colonies actually lived.

4. You _____ watch craftsmen making beautiful glass bowls.

5. Criminals _____ placed in stocks in front of the jail.

6. _____ you ever see pictures of someone with his head and hands locked in the wooden stock?

7. _____ you remember the uniformed soldiers parading around the town?

8. All the shops _____ filled with items from colonial times.

9. You _____ buy a tin whistle or a three-cornered hat.

10. The restaurants _____ filled with people enjoying delicious colonial foods.

11. _____ you ever eaten your dinner by candlelight?

12. _____ you think you would like to visit Williamsburg?

Copyright © McDougal Littell/Houghton Mifflin Company.

CHAPTER 1

Verb Phrases   *Application*

A. Writing Sentences Using Verb Phrases

Make a verb phrase by adding a helping verb to each main verb below. Then write a sentence using the verb phrase. Underline the verb phrase.

> **EXAMPLE** made
> *Eric has made six baskets in a row.*

1. play

_____

2. read

_____

3. seen

_____

4. run

_____

5. remember

_____

6. take

_____

B. Writing Using Verb Phrases

Use at least three of the following verb phrases in a story. Write the story on the lines below and underline the verb phrases that you have used.

have discovered	could make	might choose	were making
would promise	did invent	will try	can break

_____

_____

_____

_____

_____

_____

_____

_____

_____

Copyright © McDougal Littell/Houghton Mifflin Company.

Lesson 5

Compound Sentence Parts

Teaching

A **compound subject** is made up of two or more subjects that share the same verb. The subjects are joined by a conjunction, or connecting word, such as *and, or,* or *but.*

<u>Coats and jackets</u> <u>are</u> on sale at the mall.
COMPOUND SUBJECT   VERB

A **compound verb** is made up of two or more verbs that share the same subject. The verbs are joined by a conjunction such as *and, or,* or *but.*

A <u>salesclerk</u> <u>sorted and folded</u> the stack of sweaters.
SUBJECT   COMPOUND VERB

Identifying Compound Sentence Parts

In each sentence, underline the words in the compound subject or the compound verb. On the line to the right, write **CS** for compound subject or **CV** for compound verb.

EXAMPLE <u>Shoppers and store clerks</u> were busy. *CS*

1. Beth and her mom went holiday shopping at the mall. _____

2. Every parking space and aisle was filled with cars. _____

3. In the parking lot, they circled and waited for a long time. _____

4. Holiday decorations shimmered and sparkled all over the mall. _____

5. Shoppers strolled or hurried quickly from store to store. _____

6. Men and women carried huge packages in their arms. _____

7. Toys and games were stacked on large shelves. _____

8. Electronic equipment beeped and squeaked on the shelves. _____

9. Many weary shoppers paused and ate at the food court. _____

10. Knitted hats and scarves were arranged in a colorful display. _____

11. Little children clapped and shouted at the holiday puppet show. _____

12. Diamond rings and bracelets glittered in the jewelry store window. _____

13. Lindsey tried but failed in her search for a particular CD. _____

14. At the record shop, musicians played and sang popular holiday melodies. _____

15. Bill and Tom bought their in-line skates at the sporting goods store. _____

16. Books or puzzles make thoughtful holiday gifts. _____

17. A large crowd stood and watched the magic show. _____

Copyright © McDougal Littell/Houghton Mifflin Company.

CHAPTER 1

Lesson 5 · Compound Sentence Parts   *More Practice*

A. Identifying Compound Subjects and Compound Verbs

Each of the following sentences has a compound subject, a compound verb, or both. Underline the compound subjects once and the compound verbs twice.

EXAMPLE <u>Shoppers and browsers</u> <u>pick and choose</u> from the sale table.

1. My aunt studies and compares prices from many stores.
2. Teens and families eat in the food court.
3. A valuable vase slipped and fell off the counter.
4. Many shoppers stopped and looked at the new computers.
5. Antique cars and trucks are on display in the center of the mall.
6. That store buys or trades old comic books.
7. The owners or the managers repaired or repainted several shops.

B. Using Compound Subjects and Compound Verbs

Combine the sentence pairs to form a new sentence with the sentence part in parentheses. Use the conjunction—*and, or,* or *but*—that makes the most sense.

EXAMPLE Board games were on sale. Computer software was on sale too.
(compound subject)
Board games and computer software were on sale.

1. Susan went to the store for tennis shoes. Wendy also went to the store for tennis shoes. (compound subject)

_____

2. We saw several kinds of candy at the Sweet Shop. We sampled them too. (compound verb)

_____

3. At the mall ice rink, people skated to the music. People twirled around and around. (compound verb)

_____

4. Wool sweaters were hanging on a rack. Knit vests were on the same rack. (compound subject)

_____

5. At the bookstore, the bestsellers were on display. Other holiday books were on display as well. (compound subject)

_____

Copyright © McDougal Littell/Houghton Mifflin Company.

Compound Sentence Parts

Application

A. Sentence Combining with Compound Subjects and Compound Verbs

Write sentences using these compound subjects and compound verbs.

1. cash and credit

_____

2. counted and recounted

_____

3. opened and closed

_____

4. clerks and managers

_____

5. boots and shoes

_____

B. More Sentence Combining

Revise the following paragraph, using compound subjects and compound verbs to combine sentences with similar ideas. Write the new paragraph on the lines below.

Shopping at a giant computer store is an adventure. Computers in long rows cover the display area. Monitors in long rows are there too. Software programs fill many shelves. Computer manuals also fill the shelves. Customers study all the computers. They try all the computers. Finally, customers find a computer they like. They buy that computer. Many different printers are displayed in the store. Different speakers are displayed as well. Some customers compare these items. They choose the printer and speaker they like best.

_____

_____

_____

_____

_____

_____

_____

_____

Copyright © McDougal Littell/Houghton Mifflin Company.

CHAPTER 1

Kinds of Sentences   *Teaching*

A **declarative sentence** expresses a statement. It ends with a period.

> The Saint Bernard has a thick brown and white coat.

An **interrogative sentence** asks a question. It ends with a question mark.

> Is that beautiful collie your pet?

An **imperative sentence** tells or asks someone to do something. It usually ends with a period but may end with an exclamation point.

> Please feed the dog his supper.

An **exclamatory sentence** shows strong feeling. It always ends with an exclamation point.

> What a huge dog that is!

Identifying Kinds of Sentences

On the line, identify each sentence below by writing **D** for declarative, **INT** for interrogative, **IMP** for imperative, or **E** for exclamatory. Add the proper punctuation mark at the end of each sentence.

1. Give the dog a bath today _____

2. How many kinds of dogs can you name in one minute _____

3. The Chihuahua is originally from Mexico _____

4. What a cute puppy you have _____

5. How does a bloodhound's sense of smell help it find missing persons _____

6. Don't let go of the Great Dane's leash _____

7. Fetch the stick, Spot _____

8. The Irish setter has long, reddish-colored hair _____

9. Teams of huskies pull sleds over the ice and snow in Alaska _____

10. Do you know how many dogs are needed for each team _____

11. Take your dog for a walk every day _____

12. That dog tried to bite me _____

13. German shepherds make good watchdogs _____

14. Can you train your dog to roll over or sit _____

15. Please give that bone to the dog _____

Copyright © McDougal Littell/Houghton Mifflin Company.

Lesson 6

Kinds of Sentences

More Practice

Using Different Kinds of Sentences

Add the correct end punctuation to each of these sentences. Then rewrite the sentences according to the instructions in parentheses. You may have to add or delete words and change word order.

> **EXAMPLE** Your dog is playful.
> (Change to an interrogative sentence.)
> *Is your dog playful?*

1. Is that dog a good swimmer

(Change to a declarative sentence.)

_____

2. Sheepdogs can round up a herd of sheep

(Change to an interrogative sentence.)

_____

3. The Airedale terrier is a large dog

(Change to an interrogative sentence.)

_____

4. Does your dog do amazing tricks

(Change to an exclamatory sentence.)

_____

5. How gentle that dog is with little children

(Change to a declarative sentence.)

_____

6. Will you call your dog back home now

(Change to an imperative sentence.)

_____

7. What a good friend a dog can be

(Change to a declarative sentence.)

_____

Copyright © McDougal Littell/Houghton Mifflin Company.

CHAPTER 1

Kinds of Sentences

Application

A. Writing Different Kinds of Sentences

Write at least four sentences you might say if you found a dog roaming around
the halls and rooms of your school. Write at least one of each kind of sentence:
declarative, interrogative, imperative, and exclamatory. Use the correct punctuation
at the end of each sentence.

_____

_____

_____

_____

_____

_____

_____

_____

B. Writing Different Kinds of Sentences in a Diary

Imagine that you have just come back from the first meeting of an obedience class
with your dog. What might have happened there? How do you feel about your dog
now? Write a diary entry for this day. Use at least one of each kind of sentence:
declarative, interrogative, imperative, and exclamatory. Use the correct punctuation
at the end of each sentence.

_____

_____

_____

_____

_____

_____

_____

Copyright © McDougal Littell/Houghton Mifflin Company.

Lesson 7 Subjects in Unusual Order   *Teaching*

In most sentences, the subject comes before the verb. In some sentences, however, subjects may come after the verb, come in between the verb phrase, or not appear at all.

In most **questions,** the subject comes after the verb or between parts of the verb phrase.

<u>Are</u> <u>you</u> excited?   <u>Have</u> <u>you</u> <u>been</u> to the city? (*Have been* is the
VERB SUBJECT   SUBJECT   verb phrase)

The subject of a **command,** or imperative sentence, is usually *you.* Often, *you* doesn't appear in the sentence because it is understood.

<u>Study</u> the map carefully.
VERB (The **implied subject** is *You.*)

In an inverted sentence, the subject comes after the verb.

Into the car <u>climbed</u> the eager <u>family</u>.
            VERB   SUBJECT

In some sentences beginning with the words **here** or **there,** the subject follows the verb. To find the subject, look for the verb and ask *who* or *what.*

Here <u>is</u> the <u>road</u> to the city. (*What is here?*)

There <u>are</u> the <u>hotels</u> listed in the book. (*What are there?*)

Finding Subjects and Verbs in Unusual Positions

In the following sentences, underline the simple subject once and the verb or verb phrase twice. If the subject is understood, write **You** in parentheses on the line.

1. There are many museums in the city.   _____

2. Will we visit any of them?   _____

3. Here is the new science museum.   _____

4. Is the planetarium show at one o'clock?   _____

5. Look at the schedule for the time.   _____

6. Around the corner came a huge robot.   _____

7. Was Mom surprised?   _____

8. There were many visitors at the laser show.   _____

9. Are you searching for the gift shop?   _____

10. Here is an exhibit on space travel.   _____

11. Near the satellite model was a large picture of Jupiter. _____

12. Take a picture of Dad in the space suit.   _____

13. How much do you remember from that display?   _____

Copyright © McDougal Littell/Houghton Mifflin Company.

CHAPTER 1

Lesson 7 **Subjects in Unusual Order**   *More Practice*

A. Writing Sentences

In the following sentences, underline the simple subject once and the verb twice.
Then rewrite each sentence so that the subject comes before the verb.

> **EXAMPLE** Over the high fence <u>stretched</u> the tall <u>giraffe</u>.
> *The tall giraffe stretched over the high fence.*

1. Was the city zoo an interesting place?

_____

2. In the bird enclosure swooped a bald eagle.

_____

3. Near the monkey exhibit stood a large group of school children.

_____

4. Were the crocodiles in the small lake?

_____

5. On a tree branch sat a colorful parrot.

_____

B. Writing Sentences

Rewrite each sentence as an inverted or imperative sentence. You may choose to
add *Here* or *There*. If you write an imperative sentence, write **(You)** after it. Then
underline each subject once and each verb twice in your new sentence.

> **EXAMPLE** The subway traveled around the city.
> *Around the city <u>traveled</u> the <u>subway</u>.*

1. You can pay your fare at the subway entrance.

_____

2. Tall buildings reached into the blue sky.

_____

3. The art museum is at the end of the bus line.

_____

4. You must see the monument in front of City Hall.

_____

5. Many restaurants are near our hotel.

_____

Copyright © McDougal Littell/Houghton Mifflin Company.

Lesson 7 — Subjects in Unusual Order

Application

A. Revising Using Different Sentence Orders

The writer of this paragraph decided never to use the usual word order of subject before verb. In all of the paragraph's sentences, the subject is found in an unusual position or is understood. Rewrite the paragraph. Use a variety of sentence orders to improve the paragraph.

> Was our family trip to the city exciting? To many museums traveled our happy group. All over the science museum were unusual exhibits. In the planetarium was an interesting show about the stars. At the art museum were beautiful pictures. Through the zoo walked our family. Around the city by subway and bus traveled our family. Did we enjoy eating in the different restaurants around our hotel? Would we like to visit the city again someday?

_____

_____

_____

_____

_____

_____

B. Revising Using a Variety of Sentence Orders

The writer of this paragraph decided always to use the usual word order of subject before verb. Rewrite the paragraph, this time using many kinds of sentence orders. Write at least two sentences in which the subject comes before the verb. Write at least two sentences in a more unusual order, with the subject after the verb.

> Many parents and children spend time together on vacation. Some families travel to the seashore. Other families go to the mountains. A few families sail among tropical islands on large cruise ships. Some families go to exciting amusement parks. Parents and children may visit historical sites far away from home. Other families stay in their own town. They might explore nearby museums or zoos. The best vacation of all is just being together as a family.

_____

_____

_____

_____

_____

Copyright © McDougal Littell/Houghton Mifflin Company.

CHAPTER 1

Lesson 8

Complements: Subject Complements

Teaching

A complement is a word or group of words that completes the meaning of the verb.

A **subject complement** is a word or group of words that follows a linking verb and renames or describes the subject. Common **linking verbs** include forms of *be*, such as *am, is, are, was, being, been*, and *were*; and verbs such as *appear, feel, look, sound, seem*, and *taste*.

Both nouns and adjectives can serve as subject complements.

A **predicate noun** follows a linking verb and defines or renames the subject.

The painting <u>is</u> a still <u>life</u>.
     SUBJECT   PREDICATE
                 NOUN

A **predicate adjective** follows a linking verb and describes a quality of the subject.

This painting of a forest <u>is</u> unusually <u>beautiful</u>.
     SUBJECT   PREDICATE
                               ADJECTIVE

Identifying Linking Verbs and Subject Complements

In the following sentences, underline the linking verbs once and the subject complements twice. On the line, write **PA** for predicate adjective or **PN** for predicate noun.

1. Painting is one of the oldest arts. _____

2. People are a favorite subject of painters. _____

3. The subjects in early paintings were usually very important people. _____

4. Many old paintings were religious. _____

5. Other subjects were historical or mythical figures. _____

6. Later, common people became the subjects of paintings. _____

7. Sometimes, the people in paintings look very realistic. _____

8. Other paintings are imaginative. _____

9. The people and scenery seem dreamlike. _____

10. Another popular subject is nature. _____

11. Landscapes and seascapes are paintings of our natural world. _____

12. Still lifes are pictures of objects. _____

13. These subjects look quite detailed. _____

14. Some paintings become huge, covering whole walls. _____

15. Other paintings are tiny. _____

Copyright © McDougal Littell/Houghton Mifflin Company.

Name _____ Date _____

Lesson 8 # Complements: Subject Complements   *More Practice*

A. Identifying Types of Subject Complements

In each of the following sentences, underline the linking verb once and the subject complement twice. Then, on the line, write **PN** if the subject complement is a predicate noun or **PA** if it is a predicate adjective.

EXAMPLE The lives of many artists <u>were</u> <u>interesting</u>. *PA*

1. Michelangelo was an artistic genius. _____

2. His styles of art were quite different. _____

3. Michelangelo became a sculptor. _____

4. His large, marble statues appear lifelike. _____

5. Many of his statues feel incredibly smooth. _____

6. Michelangelo became famous for his paintings. _____

7. His paintings in the Sistine Chapel look magnificent. _____

8. His career as an architect was challenging. _____

9. The dome of St. Peter's Church was his plan. _____

10. In his later years, Michelangelo became a poet. _____

B. Using Subject Complements

Complete each sentence below. First complete it with a predicate noun. Then complete it with a predicate adjective.

EXAMPLE The artist is *my uncle*.
The artist is <u>talented</u>.

1. The painting is _____.

   The painting is _____.

2. The colors are _____.

   The colors are _____.

3. The dog in the painting is _____.

   The dog in the painting is _____.

4. The painting's setting is _____.

   The painting's setting is _____.

Copyright © McDougal Littell/Houghton Mifflin Company.

CHAPTER 1

Lesson 8

Complements: Subject Complements *Application*

A. Writing Subject Complements

Rewrite each of the numbered sentences in the passage below with a new subject complement. Underline your new subject complement. If it is a predicate noun, write **PN** in parentheses after the sentence. If it is a predicate adjective, write **PA.**

(1) My favorite form of art is sculpture. (2) The work of art that I wish I owned is a statue of a young dancer. (3) It looks beautiful. (4) When I look at that artwork, I feel happy. (5) It is truly a masterpiece. (6) The life of an artist must be very satisfying.

1. _____

2. _____

3. _____

4. _____

5. _____

6. _____

B. Writing with Subject Complements

Imagine that you have just visited a museum where you saw some unusual works of art. Write six sentences about your museum visit and what you saw there. Three of the sentences should have predicate adjectives. Three should have predicate nouns.

1. _____

_____

2. _____

_____

3. _____

_____

4. _____

_____

5. _____

_____

6. _____

_____

Copyright © McDougal Littell/Houghton Mifflin Company.

Lesson 9 — Complements: Objects of Verbs
Teaching

Action verbs often need complements called direct objects and indirect objects to complete their meaning.

A **direct object** is a word or a group of words that names the receiver of the action of an action verb. It answers the question *what* or *whom*.

    Dad read the <u>comics</u>. (*What* did Dad read?)

An **indirect object** is a word or group of words that tells *to what* or *to whom*, or *for whom* or *for what* an action is done. The indirect object usually comes between the verb and the direct object. Verbs that are often followed by an indirect object include *ask, bring, give, hand, lend, make, offer, send, show, teach, tell,* and *write*.

    Dad read his <u>daughter</u> the comics. (*To whom* did Dad read the comics?)

Recognizing Objects of Verbs

In each sentence, if the underlined word is a direct object, write **DO** on the line. If it is an indirect object, write **IO**.

    EXAMPLE The diver found a <u>shipwreck</u>. *DO*

1. The detective finally solved the <u>mystery</u>. _____

2. The campers cooked their <u>food</u> over an open fire. _____

3. The loud music gave <u>me</u> a headache. _____

4. The rabbit in *Alice in Wonderland* carries a <u>watch</u>. _____

5. Andrea showed my <u>family</u> the photographs from her trip. _____

6. We offered <u>Jim</u> a ride to the game. _____

7. The electric eel stuns its <u>enemies</u> with an electric shock. _____

8. Remember to send your <u>hostess</u> a thank-you note. _____

9. Mr. Weld baked his <u>daughter</u> a birthday cake. _____

10. The monkeys climbed the tall <u>trees</u> in the rain forest. _____

11. Candice told her <u>sister</u> a secret. _____

12. You can rent <u>videos</u> at that store. _____

13. The Bureau of the Mint manufactures all <u>coins</u> in the United States. _____

14. Enrique taught his <u>dog</u> a new trick. _____

15. Imagine a <u>city</u> under the sea. _____

Copyright © McDougal Littell/Houghton Mifflin Company.

Lesson 9 Complements: Objects of Verbs   *More Practice*

A. Identifying Objects of Verbs

Identify the function of the boldfaced word in each sentence below. Write **DO** for direct object or **IO** for indirect object. If the word is not the direct object or the indirect object write **N**.

1. Lighthouses are **towers** with extremely strong lights. _____

2. The bright lights guide **ships** at night or in fog. _____

3. Lighthouses show **sailors** the safe routes around rocks and reefs. _____

4. Lighthouses also use foghorns and send **navigators** loud warning sounds. _____

5. Lighthouses give **sailors** confidence as they approach land. _____

6. People have been building **lighthouses** for thousands of years. _____

7. Ancient Egyptians started **fires** on hills to guide ships. _____

8. Later, the Egyptians completed the **Pharos of Alexandria,** the tallest lighthouse ever constructed. _____

9. In the past, keepers operated all **lighthouses.** _____

10. Now, lighthouses are **beacons** run by computers. _____

B. Using Indirect Objects

Underline the direct object in each sentence below. Then rewrite each sentence, adding an indirect object. Use a different indirect object for every sentence.

1. Lauren sent invitations to her party.

_____

2. The tennis pro gave a few lessons.

_____

3. The server offered some coffee.

_____

4. Dana wrote a long letter.

_____

5. The confused student asked a question.

_____

Copyright © McDougal Littell/Houghton Mifflin Company.

Lesson 9

Complements: Objects of Verbs

Application

CHAPTER 1

A. Using Objects of Verbs

Choose one word from each list below to complete each sentence. Use each word only once. Each sentence should have both an indirect object and a direct object. If you wish, you can add words to make the sentences more interesting.

Use as indirect object	Use as direct object	
the mayor	some lemonade	
his nephew	a letter	
their friends	two new words	
the class	a football	
his grandfather	some muffins	
her family	postcards	
her parakeet	a difficult question	
her guests	a movie	

1. Uncle Ted gave_____.

2. Ms. Dwyer offered _____.

3. The reporter asked_____.

4. The tourists sent _____.

5. Brenda baked _____.

6. The social studies teacher showed _____.

7. Kevin wrote_____.

8. Roberta taught _____.

B. Writing Sentences with Objects of Verbs

Complete each sentence with a direct and an indirect object. Use a different direct and indirect object in every sentence.

EXAMPLE Mr. Martin taught *his students a new song*.

1. The banker will lend _____.

2. My aunt wrote _____.

3. The mail carrier brought _____.

4. The artist showed _____.

5. The salesclerk gave _____.

Copyright © McDougal Littell/Houghton Mifflin Company.

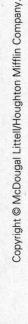

CHAPTER 1

Lesson 10 Fragments and Run-Ons   *Teaching*

Sentence fragments and run-on sentences are writing errors that can make your writing difficult to understand.

A **sentence fragment** is part of a sentence that is written as if it were a complete sentence. A sentence fragment is missing a subject, a predicate, or both.

> **Fragments** The Maya, a Native American people. (missing a predicate)
> Developed a magnificent civilization. (missing a subject)
> In southern Mexico and Central America. (missing both)
>
> **Revision**   The Maya, a Native American people, developed a magnificent civilization in southern Mexico and Central America.

A **run-on sentence** is two or more sentences written as if they were a single sentence. When you combine two sentences with a conjunction, use a comma before the conjunction.

> **Run-on** The Maya lived in Central America their descendants still live there.
> **Revision** The Maya lived in Central America, and their descendants still live there.

Identifying Sentences, Sentence Fragments, and Run-Ons

On the line to the right of each word group below, write **CS, F,** or **RO** to identify the word group as a complete sentence, a fragment, or a run-on sentence.

1. Existed as long ago as B.C. 2000.

2. The Maya created hundreds of great cities out of stone.

3. Most of the Maya were farmers they came to the cities to attend festivals.

4. Only priests, nobles, rulers, and officials.

5. The Maya built a network of roads these roads encouraged trade between groups of people throughout Central America.

6. In the tropical rain forests of northern Guatemala.

7. They were very advanced in science, mathematics, and art.

8. The Maya had a game that resembled basketball the players hit a rubber ball through a hoop with their elbows and hips.

9. Used astronomy to develop a calendar.

10. A Mayan calendar had 365 days.

11. The Maya had no overall ruler or government every city was independent.

12. Why the Mayan civilization collapsed.

Copyright © McDougal Littell/Houghton Mifflin Company.

Name _____ Date _____

Lesson 10

Fragments and Run-Ons

More Practice

A. Identifying and Correcting Fragments and Run-Ons

On the line after each word group below, write **CS**, **F**, or **RO** to identify the word group as a complete sentence, a fragment, or a run-on sentence. Then rewrite each fragment or run-on as one or more correct sentences. Add sentence parts as needed.

1. It's cold today remember to bring your jacket. _____

_____

2. Down the street. _____

_____

3. Cary is a drummer in a band. _____

_____

4. The play begins at 2:00 we had better hurry. _____

_____

5. Hundreds of people in the stands. _____

_____

B. Correcting Fragments and Run-ons

Rewrite this paragraph, correcting each fragment and run-on. You may add words to any fragment to make it a sentence or combine it with another sentence. To correct a run-on, you may either separate the sentences or join them correctly.

> The Aztecs ruled a mighty empire in Mexico. During the 1400s and 1500s. Aztecs had an advanced civilization they built cities as big as any in Europe. The Aztecs built a huge city. On an island in a lake. A population of one hundred thousand people. Conquered other cities in Mexico. The conquered people sent food as a tribute they also provided gold and silver.

_____

_____

_____

_____

_____

_____

_____

_____

Copyright © McDougal Littell/Houghton Mifflin Company.

Lesson 10

Fragments and Run-Ons

Application

A. Proofreading for Fragments and Run-Ons

Rewrite this paragraph, correcting each fragment and run-on. You may add words to any fragment to make it a sentence, or combine it with another sentence. To correct a run-on, you may either separate the sentences or join them correctly.

> The main food of the Aztecs. A thin cornmeal pancake called a *tlaxcalli*. In Spanish, this food is called a *tortilla* the Aztecs wrapped these pancakes around meat and vegetables to make *tacos*. Created a drink made with chocolate. This was one of their favorite drinks only the wealthy could afford it often. These foods, developed by the Aztecs. Have become popular all over the world.

_____

_____

_____

_____

_____

_____

B. Recognizing and Revising Fragments and Run-ons

Read these notes one student wrote to use in a report. First figure out what the writer was going to say, and then use the information to write a paragraph. Use complete sentences instead of fragments and run-on sentences. Add any words that you need to make the paragraph understandable. Use a separate piece of paper, if nexessary.

> Braille. A code of small raised dots on paper that can be read by touch. Louis Braille, a 15-year-old French student. At the National Institute for the Blind in Paris. Developed this raised dot system in 1824. Braille worked out an alphabet and numerals using this system he even figured out how to use the raised dots to write music. Read this system by running their fingers over the dots. Each Braille page has words written on both sides of the paper, dots on one side do not interfere with the dots printed on the other side. This system of writing for the blind. Named after Louis Braille.

_____

_____

_____

_____

_____

Copyright © McDougal Littell/Houghton Mifflin Company.

Copyright © McDougal Littell/Houghton Mifflin Company.

Lesson 1

What Is a Noun?

Teaching

A **noun** is a word that names a person, place, thing, or idea. Examples are *doctor, hospital, medicine,* and *recovery.*

A **common noun** is a general name for a person, place, thing, or idea. A proper noun is the name of a particular one. For example, *hospital* is a common noun; *Pittsburgh Hospital* is a proper noun. Only proper nouns need to be capitalized.

A. Identifying Nouns

Underline all the nouns in the following sentences.

1. Doctors get satisfaction when their patients recover quickly.
2. Scout troops sometimes make trips to local hospitals.
3. Dr. Percy Julian believed that soybeans had great value.
4. That nurse graduated from Central Nursing Institute.
5. The clinic in our neighborhood is open every Saturday.
6. Brenda Marshall is a nurse in a busy unit.
7. Mrs. Johnson joined her family in the lounge of the hospital.
8. Dr. Stern can calm the worries of nervous patients.
9. My little brother had his tonsils removed by Dr. Bradley.
10. The staff of doctors at Grant Hospital are dependable.
11. Nurse Thompson will measure your height and weight.

B. Identifying Common and Proper Nouns

If the boldfaced noun is common, write **C** on the line to the right. If it is proper, write **P** on the line.

1. The usher in the theater shined his **flashlight** on the empty seats. _____

2. T. S. Eliot wrote a poem about a cat named **Macavity.** _____

3. **Dr. Martin Luther King, Jr.,** fought for equality and freedom. _____

4. In the myths of ancient Greece, **Cerberus** was a watchdog with three heads. _____

5. To some Native Americans, the **buffalo** is a symbol of good fortune. _____

6. **Spiders** spin webs to catch insects. _____

7. The pioneers who traveled to **California** in covered wagons faced many dangers. _____

8. Alyssa wrote a story about a space creature from **Mars.** _____

9. The visitors admired the **statues** outside the museum. _____

CHAPTER 2

CHAPTER 2

Lesson 1

What is a Noun?

More Practice

A. Identifying Nouns

Underline all the nouns in each of the following sentences. On the lines below, write the nouns that match the descriptions in parentheses.

1. Dr. Weber stopped at the pharmacy.

(proper) _____ (common) _____

2. The generosity of Mrs. Fairfield was much appreciated.

(proper) _____ (abstract) _____

3. Our class sent a get-well card to Mrs. Turner.

(proper) _____ (common) _____

(common) _____

4. A group visited patients at Sunshine Home.

(proper) _____ (common) _____

(common) _____

5. The cafeteria at Fillmore Hospital has delicious food.

(proper) _____ (common) _____

(common) _____

B. Using Nouns

Complete each sentence with one of the nouns from the list below.

relief	Harlan Hospital	bouquet	water
bed	Maple Street	uncle	Green Pharmacy

1. Mike's _____ came to the hospital to visit him.

2. Columbia Hospital is at the corner of Green Avenue and
_____.

3. Beth sat up in the _____ while Mom adjusted the TV.

4. "May I please have a glass of _____?" she asked.

5. My family felt _____ when the doctor said I could go home.

6. An aide delivered a _____ of flowers to Kim's room.

7. _____ has evening visiting hours.

8. We got our prescription filled at the _____.

Copyright © McDougal Littell/Houghton Mifflin Company.

Lesson 1 # What Is a Noun? *Application*

A. Using Nouns

Rewrite each sentence, replacing the boldfaced common noun with a proper noun.
You may need to change some words, such as *a, an,* and *the.*

> EXAMPLE That **dog** belongs to my friend.
> *Sir Benchley belongs to my friend.*

1. The team met at a **restaurant.**

_____

2. The **mayor** visited Austin Middle School.

_____

3. My cousin shops at that **store.**

_____

4. That **road** is the busiest street in the city.

_____

5. Our **market** sells my favorite cereal at a good price.

_____

B. Using Nouns in Writing

Write a short paragraph describing your favorite book. Mention the title, some of
the characters' names, and what you like about the book. Include at least three
proper nouns and three common nouns. Underline the common nouns once and
the proper nouns twice.

_____

_____

_____

_____

_____

_____

_____

_____

_____

Copyright © McDougal Littell/Houghton Mifflin Company.

CHAPTER 2

CHAPTER 2

Lesson 2 Singular and Plural Nouns

Teaching

A **singular noun** names one person, place, thing, or idea. A **plural noun** names more than one person, place, thing, or idea.

> One <u>author</u> wrote a great <u>book</u>. (singular nouns)
> Some <u>authors</u> write a number of <u>books</u>. (plural nouns)

This chart shows the usual ways to form the plurals of nouns.

Singular	Rule	Sample Plural
shirt, hat	Add -*s* to most nouns.	shirts, hats
bush, mix	Add -*es* to nouns ending in *s*, *sh*, *ch*, *x*, or *z*.	bushes, mixes
radio echo, hero	Add -*s* to most nouns that end in *o*. Add -*es* to a few nouns that end in *o*.	radios echoes, heroes
pony, fly monkey, day	Change the *y* to an *i* and add -*es* to most nouns ending in *y*. If a vowel comes before the *y*, add -*s*.	ponies, flies monkeys, days
shelf, knife roof, cuff	Change the *f* to a *v* and add -*es* to most nouns that end in *f* or *fe*. Add -*s* to a few nouns that end in *f* or *fe*.	shelves, knives roofs, cuffs
sheep, tuna	Some nouns keep the same spelling.	sheep, tuna
woman, foot	The plural forms of some nouns are irregular.	women, feet

A. Identifying Plural Forms of Nouns

In each sentence, underline only the plural nouns.

1. Cows take good care of their newborn calves.

2. The ponies ran freely in the fields.

3. Cowboys work hard at their daily chores.

4. The noises made by geese woke me up.

5. Some parties include hayrides.

B. Correcting Errors in Plural Nouns

In each sentence, one plural noun is boldfaced. If it has been formed incorrectly, write the correct form on the line. If it is correct, write **Correct** on the line.

1. What are your favorite **activitys** on the farm? _____

2. Pony rides are fun for the **childs**. _____

3. Mom enjoys growing **tomatos** in her garden. _____

4. Dad caught several **fish** for supper. _____

5. Some farmers worry that **foxs** will harm the chickens. _____

Copyright © McDougal Littell/Houghton Mifflin Company.

Lesson 2

Singular and Plural Nouns

More Practice

A. Identifying Plural Forms of Nouns

In each sentence, underline only the plural nouns.

1. Our families will spend seven days on a farm.
2. The children will help tend pigs and sheep.
3. I like to hear the echoes of their happy cries.
4. Farmers are always busy with their crops and animals.
5. My sisters pack tomatoes into boxes to be shipped to markets.
6. Most nights on the farm are spent telling stories by the fireplace.

B. Correcting Errors in Plural Nouns

In each sentence, underline the plural noun that has been formed incorrectly. Write the correctly spelled plural on the line.

1. Some people have interesting hobbys.   _____

2. Many woman enjoy making patchwork quilts.   _____

3. Grandma has boxs filled with cotton squares.   _____

4. Her fabrics are stored on special shelfs.   _____

5. She makes quilts for all the new babys.   _____

6. Every family sends her photoes of the newborns.   _____

7. Both of my uncleses are excellent woodworkers.   _____

8. They use carving knifes of various sizes.   _____

9. Uncle Sam paints his carved objectes.   _____

10. He has many paintbrushs for his work.   _____

C. Using Plural Nouns

Form the plural of the given nouns. Then use all three plurals in a single sentence.

1. wife _____ city _____ photo _____

   _____

2. boy _____ sandwich _____ loaf _____

   _____

3. goose _____ field _____ grass _____

   _____

Copyright © McDougal Littell/Houghton Mifflin Company.

Lesson 2

Singular and Plural Nouns

Application

A. Using Plural Nouns

In the following sentences, decide whether the plural nouns have been formed correctly. Rewrite every sentence with the correct noun forms.

1. Cowboys on ranchs have many dutys to perform.

_____

2. They sometimes use doges to round up the cattles.

_____

3. Old television programs showed cowboys as heros.

_____

4. Peoples laughed at some of the activitys.

_____

5. Rodeoes could be dangerous for many mans.

_____

6. Bronco rideres had to keep their foots firmly in the stirrups.

_____

7. A cowboy's skilles are admired by rodeo fans in many countrys.

_____

B. Using Plural Nouns in Writing

Your family is making plans to spend one year living in another country. The climate will be different, and you will be attending a new school. Write a short paragraph describing how you will prepare yourself for this adventure. Underline at least five plural nouns in your paragraph.

_____

_____

_____

_____

_____

_____

_____

_____

_____

Copyright © McDougal Littell/Houghton Mifflin Company.

CHAPTER 2

Lesson 3

Possessive Nouns   *Teaching*

The **possessive** form of a noun shows ownership or relationship. Use an apostrophe to show possession. For example, *Mom's* car (ownership); *brother's* friend (relationship).

You may use possessive nouns in place of longer phrases.

> Head coverings are used for the protection of the beekeeper.
> Head coverings are used for the <u>beekeeper's</u> protection.

The following chart shows the usual ways to form the plurals of possessive nouns.

Noun		Rule	Possessive
Singular:	dog	Add an apostrophe and -s.	dog's bone
Plural ending in -s:	spiders	Add an apostrophe.	spiders' webs
Plurals not ending in -s:	children	Add an apostrophe and -s.	children's caps

A. Identifying Possessive Nouns

Underline each possessive noun. Above it, write **S** for a singular noun and **P** for a plural noun.

1. That wasp's sting should have an adult's attention.

2. Termites' nests are the most amazing sights!

3. Moths' bodies are plumper than butterflies' bodies.

4. Those children's lunches are being attacked by ants.

5. A queen bee's life span is about four years.

B. Using Possessive Nouns

In each sentence, a possessive noun is boldfaced. If it has been formed incorrectly, write the correct form on the line. If it is correct, write **Correct** on the line.

1. Can you describe a **grasshoppers'** wings? _____

2. Some insects are **farmers'** friends because they eat
harmful insects. _____

3. A **ladybugs'** diet is chiefly insect pests and their eggs. _____

4. Like the leaders of bees, **wasp's** leaders are known as queens. _____

5. Most tent **caterpillar's** colonies are found among tree branches. _____

6. You might be surprised at **butterflies's** appetites. _____

7. A bulldog **ant's** body grows to a length of one inch. _____

Copyright © McDougal Littell/Houghton Mifflin Company.

Lesson 3
Possessive Nouns
More Practice

A. Identifying Possessive Nouns

Underline the possessive noun in each sentence. On the line, write **S** for singular or **P** for plural to describe the possessive noun.

1. Where does a firefly's light come from? _____

2. Supervisors of children's camps are aware of insect dangers. _____

3. Asia's caterpillars make cocoons out of one thread. _____

4. Honeybees' homes are called colonies. _____

5. Every honeybee's job is important to the success of the colony. _____

6. An aphid's body might or might not have wings. _____

7. Aphids' enormous appetites have caused widespread loss of crops such as potatoes, cabbages, and apples. _____

8. Every insect's behavior is instinctive; it knows how to act and what to do from the moment it is born. _____

B. Correcting Errors in Possessive Nouns

In each sentence underline the possessive noun. If it has been formed incorrectly, write it correctly on the line. If it is correct, write **Correct** on the line.

1. A bees' stinger is used for its protection. _____

2. Some soldier ant's mouths are so big, they cannot feed themselves. _____

3. Homeowners's fears grow when they see signs of termite activity. _____

4. Moth's colors help them blend in with their surroundings. _____

5. Those women's recipes are for honey cakes and honey breads. _____

6. Green aphids's favorite hiding places are green plant stems. _____

7. Caterpillar damage can ruin a farmers' crop. _____

8. How vivid that ladybugs' spots are! _____

9. Male crickets' chirps are made by rubbing their forewings together. _____

10. Cricket's relatives are locusts and grasshoppers. _____

CHAPTER 2

Copyright © McDougal Littell/Houghton Mifflin Company.

Copyright © McDougal Littell/Houghton Mifflin Company.

Name _____ Date _____

Possessive Nouns

Application

A. Using Possessive Nouns

Use a possessive noun to shorten each phrase. Then use the new phrase in a sentence.

> **EXAMPLE** the barking of a dog *the dog's barking*
> *The dog's barking kept me awake all night.*

1. the flight of the geese _____

_____

2. the cries of the children _____

_____

3. wool from the sheep _____

_____

4. the cottage of the family _____

_____

5. the sting of a wasp _____

_____

6. the wings of butterflies _____

_____

B. Using Possessives in Writing

Imagine that you recently spent an afternoon exploring a relative's attic. Write a letter to a cousin telling him or her about the interesting items you found. Mention some items and their original owners, such as grandparents, aunts, or uncles. Underline at least five possessive nouns in your letter.

_____

_____

_____

_____

_____

_____

_____

CHAPTER 2

Lesson 4 # Nouns and Their Jobs   *Teaching*

Nouns can have several different jobs in sentences.

As a **subject,** the noun tells whom or what the sentence is about.

   Our <u>family</u> enjoys the circus.

As a **complement,** the noun completes the meaning of a verb. Nouns that are complements may be **predicate nouns, direct objects,** or **indirect objects.** The following chart shows the ways nouns are used as complements.

Predicate noun	renames or defines the subject after a linking verb	The circus is a special **event.**
Direct object	names the receiver of the action of the action verb	We took **pictures** of the clown.
Indirect object	tells *to whom or what* or *for whom or what* an action is done	Dad gave **Matthew** his camera.

A noun also may be used as an **object of the preposition.**

   Holly carried extra film in her <u>backpack</u>.
   (The preposition is *in*. The object of the preposition is the noun *backpack*.)

Identifying Subjects, Complements, and Objects of Prepositions

In each sentence, identify the word in bold type. On the blank, write **S** for subject, **PN** for predicate noun. **DO** for direct object, **IO** for indirect object, or **OP** for object of the preposition.

1. In the old days, circus performers traveled in **wagons.** _____

2. The **people** in towns along the way were excited about the circus. _____

3. Outdoor **stages** were often set up in the town center. _____

4. Later, trains transported the **performers** and their families. _____

5. Huge tents were used for the **performances.** _____

6. Circus animals probably like the **applause** of audiences. _____

7. A bareback rider is a skilled **performer.** _____

8. One clown told **Dad** a funny joke. _____

9. The silliest clown is the **fellow** wearing those floppy shoes. _____

10. Those dogs carried the **sticks** back to their trainer. _____

11. Each **clown** has a special trademark expression all his or her own. _____

12. Elephants are **part** of the circus maintenance crew. _____

Copyright © McDougal Littell/Houghton Mifflin Company.

Lesson 4 **Nouns and Their Jobs**   *More Practice*

A. Identifying Nouns and Their Jobs

Find the noun that does the job described in parentheses. Write the noun on the line to the right.

1. An animal trainer must be a patient person. (predicate noun)   _____

2. Albert Court was a famous French animal trainer. (subject)   _____

3. He used kindness with his animals. (direct object)   _____

4. Sometimes lions can seem friendly and harmless. (subject)   _____

5. Their sharp claws can injure people. (direct object)   _____

6. The trainer offered his animals treats in exchange for good behavior. (indirect object)   _____

7. Circus man John Ringling North pictured elephants in a kind of ballet. (direct object)   _____

8. He gave George Ballanchine the job of choreographer. (indirect object)   _____

9. A famous composer wrote the music for the ballet. (direct object)   _____

10. The ballet was a success. (predicate noun)   _____

B. Using Nouns as Objects of Prepositions

Underline the prepositional phrase in each sentence. On the blank line write the noun that is the object of the preposition.

EXAMPLE: The clown <u>with the sad face</u> rode a tricycle. *face*

1. Trapeze artists are masters of the air.

_____

2. Direct from the jungle come the tigers and the lions.

_____

3. Vendors stroll through the stands selling popcorn and soda.

_____

4. The sign above the circus entrance promises excitement and thrills.

_____

5. A talented young woman rides two horses around the ring.

_____

Copyright © McDougal Littell/Houghton Mifflin Company.

Lesson 4

Nouns and Their Jobs

Application

A. Identifying Nouns Used as Complements

Underline each subject in the following sentences. Then identify every boldfaced word as a predicate noun **(PN)**, a direct object **(DO)**, or an indirect object **(IO)**.

1. Clowns receive **applause** from people of all ages.   _____

2. The clown smiled and gave **Mom** a balloon.   _____

3. Emmett Kelly was a great pantomime **artist**.   _____

4. That sad-faced clown used a **broom** to sweep up a spotlight.   _____

5. The spotlight became only a **dot**.   _____

6. Kelly gave the **audience** many wonderful performances.   _____

7. That little car holds so many **people!**   _____

8. Janine loaned **Heidi** her binoculars to see the jugglers.   _____

9. My father is the circus's biggest **booster**.   _____

B. Using Nouns as Objects of Prepositions

Complete each phrase with a noun that is acting as the object of the preposition. Then write a sentence using the entire prepositional phrase.

EXAMPLE before the <u>show</u>
Before the show the jugglers practiced their act.

1. under the _____

_____

2. across a _____

_____

3. around the _____

_____

4. behind the _____

_____

5. after the _____

_____

Copyright © McDougal Littell/Houghton Mifflin Company.

Lesson 1

What Is a Pronoun?   *Teaching*

A **pronoun** is a word that is used in place of a noun or another pronoun. The word that a personal pronoun refers to is called its **antecedent.**

Personal pronouns change their forms to reflect **person, number,** and **case.**

Person Personal pronouns have different forms for first person, second person, and third person.

Number Pronouns can be singular or plural.

Case Personal pronouns change their forms depending on how they are used in a sentence. Each pronoun has three cases: subject, object, and possessive.

		Subject	Object	Possessive
Singular	*First Person*	I	me	my, mine
	Second Person	you	you	your, yours
	Third Person	he, she, it	him, her, it	his, her, hers, its
Plural	*First Person*	we	us	our, ours
	Second Person	you	you	your, yours
	Third Person	they	them	their, theirs

Finding Personal Pronouns

Underline each personal pronoun in the following sentences.

1. Have you ever heard of the Underground Railroad?
2. It played an important part in our history.
3. What we call the Underground Railroad was actually a system that helped slaves escape to freedom.
4. Its secret way of moving slaves northward gave the Underground Railroad its name.
5. The slaves traveled by night with their few possessions.
6. During the day, kind and brave people sheltered and fed them.
7. It was a long, dangerous journey to the North and freedom.
8. If escaped slaves were caught, they would be sent back to their masters.
9. Returned slaves knew terrible punishments awaited them.
10. Many people are famous for helping their fellow human beings during this time.
11. Levi Coffin used his home as a station on the Underground Railroad.
12. He helped more than 3,000 people escape.
13. Harriet Tubman relied on her skills as a guide; she led many groups of slaves to freedom.
14. I think all Americans should know about the Underground Railroad.

Copyright © McDougal Littell/Houghton Mifflin Company.

CHAPTER 3

Lesson 1

What Is a Pronoun?

More Practice

A. Finding Personal Pronouns

Underline each personal pronoun in the following sentences.

1. What does the word *abolitionist* mean to you?
2. An abolitionist spoke out against slavery before and during our Civil War.
3. Sojourner Truth was a well-known abolitionist in her day.
4. She was a former slave named Isabella Baumfree.
5. Her stirring speeches on slavery convinced many people of its evils.
6. She met with Abraham Lincoln when he was president.
7. Not only was Frederick Douglass an abolitionist, but he was also a conductor on the Underground Railroad.
8. Through his efforts many slaves escaped from their masters.
9. He was a noted author and published his own newspaper, the *North Star*.
10. His writings can still inspire us today.
11. We owe a debt of gratitude to people like them.
12. They made Americans aware of a terrible problem in our country.

B. Using Personal Pronouns

Replace the underlined nouns in this paragraph with personal pronouns. Write the pronouns on the lines below. Capitalize the pronoun if it comes at the beginning of a sentence.

Harriet Beecher Stowe lived in the United States during the Civil War. **(1)** <u>Harriet Beecher Stowe</u> was an author who felt strongly about the issue of slavery. **(2)** <u>Harriet Beecher Stowe's</u> most famous book was *Uncle Tom's Cabin*. **(3)** <u>Uncle Tom's Cabin</u> was a novel that told a sad story about slaves and the **(4)** <u>slaves'</u> harsh treatment by the **(5)** <u>slaves'</u> masters. Many people, especially the Southern slaveowners, were upset by the book. **(6)** <u>People</u> protested what they felt was an unfair picture of slavery in *Uncle Tom's Cabin*. Other Americans became inspired by the book. **(7)** <u>These Americans</u> realized more than ever before that slavery was wrong. *Uncle Tom's Cabin* turned **(8)** <u>Americans</u> against the evils of slavery. Now the book and the **(9)** <u>book's</u> author are a part of American history.

1. _____   6. _____

2. _____   7. _____

3. _____   8. _____

4. _____   9. _____

5. _____

Copyright © McDougal Littell/Houghton Mifflin Company.

CHAPTER 3

Lesson 1 # What Is a Pronoun?   *Application*

A. Using Personal Pronouns

Rewrite this paragraph, using personal pronouns to replace some of the nouns that have been used too often. Write your revised paragraph on the lines below.

> Sarah and Angelina Grimke were sisters. Although Sarah and Angelina Grimke were born in South Carolina, a part of the country that favored slavery, both sisters were active in the abolitionist movement. Sarah moved away from the South to Philadelphia because Sarah strongly believed slavery was wrong. Later, Sarah's sister, Angelina, also moved to Philadelphia. The sisters joined antislavery groups who shared the sisters' beliefs. Both Sarah and Angelina wrote pamphlets against slavery. The words in the pamphlets were stirring, and the words convinced more and more people to fight slavery.

_____

_____

_____

_____

_____

_____

_____

B. Using Personal Pronouns in a Diary

Imagine that you are a runaway slave trying to escape to freedom. Write a diary entry for today. Be sure to use a variety of personal pronouns.

_____

_____

_____

_____

_____

_____

_____

_____

Copyright © McDougal Littell/Houghton Mifflin Company.

Lesson 2

Subject Pronouns

Teaching

A **subject pronoun** is used as the subject of a sentence or as a predicate pronoun after a linking verb.

Subject Pronouns	
Singular	**Plural**
I	we
you	you
he, she, it	they

Use the **subject case** of a pronoun when the pronoun is the subject of a sentence. Remember that a pronoun can be part of a compound subject.

Subject   Sixth graders helped with the art fair. They worked very hard. (*They* replaces *Sixth graders.*)

Compound subject Ramon and I decided to paint a mural.

Use the subject case for predicate pronouns. A **predicate pronoun** follows a linking verb and renames, or refers to, the subject. Remember that the most common linking verbs are forms of the verb *be* and include *is, am, are, was, were, been, has been, have been, can be, will be, could be,* and *should be.*

Predicate pronoun   A wonderful painter was he.

A. Identifying Subject Pronouns

Underline all the subject pronouns in the following sentences.

1. Ms. Edmond's class and I will collect the art.
2. We will label each drawing that is entered in the fair.
3. Will you help Paula set up display easels?
4. We keep the easels in the storage room.
5. After the easels are arranged, you and she may help with other jobs.
6. Mr. Strong's class and he might carry the pottery to the art fair.
7. It is very heavy.

B. Using Subject Pronouns

Underline the correct pronoun to complete each sentence.

1. During the art fair, Greg and (I, me) acted as guides.
2. Hundreds of pictures were on display; (they, them) were beautiful.
3. (He, him) and I helped visitors around the auditorium.
4. When visitors arrived, (they, them) were impressed with the quality of the work.
5. Very busy guides were (us, we).
6. Is (her, she) the one who drew that scene?
7. While Lonnie was at the fair, (him, he) viewed the pottery exhibit.
8. Will you and (her, she) help with the plans for next year's fair?

Copyright © McDougal Littell/Houghton Mifflin Company.

CHAPTER 3

Lesson 2 **Subject Pronouns**   *More Practice*

A. Using Subject Pronouns

In each sentence, underline the pronoun that completes each sentence correctly.

1. Although Tiffany and Sue liked the art fair, (them, they) could not stay long.
2. Sue entered a drawing of her cat; (she, her) hoped to win a prize.
3. Both Bob and (me, I) thought Sue's drawing should win.
4. (He, Him) liked two other pictures of cats.
5. (Them, They) were painted in bright colors.
6. A local artist judged the entries, and (he, him) awarded the prizes too.
7. "Did (I, me) win a ribbon for my pottery?" asked Carl.
8. Another boy and (him, he) won blue ribbons for their work.
9. When Sue's name was called, (we, us) were very excited.
10. A winner of a gold ribbon was (she, her).
11. When all the winners were announced, (they, them) were congratulated by our principal.
12. (We, Us) were glad the art fair was such a success.

B. Choosing Subject Pronouns

Fill in the blanks in the following sentences with appropriate subject pronouns. Vary the pronouns you use, but do not use the pronoun *you.*

1. _____ decided to write a story about his pet gerbil.

2. Lucy and _____ took the books to the library.

3. _____ stood on the stairs for our class picture.

4. The leads in the play will be Latisha and _____.

5. Although that team's players were shorter, _____ won the basketball game.

6. _____ wrote the report on my new computer.

7. When the glass fell, _____ shattered into many sharp pieces.

8. Will Don or _____ play the flute solo at the concert?

9. The co-captains of the team are Terrell and _____.

10. When the sanitation workers stopped at our house,_____ picked up the old sofa.

Copyright © McDougal Littell/Houghton Mifflin Company.

CHAPTER 3

Lesson 2 **Subject Pronouns** *Application*

A. Proofreading

Proofread the following story to make sure that subject pronouns have been used in the right places. When you find a pronoun used incorrectly, cross it out. Then insert this proofreading symbol ⅃ and write the correct pronoun above it.

An art fair at school is always fun for art teachers. At an art fair, them and their students can show off their artistic skills. Pictures are everywhere. One artist may use oil paint for a landscape, but him or her might use watercolors on the next piece. Some artists paint portraits because they like to draw people. My friend and I enjoy trying new techniques. Perhaps him or me will work with cloth or yarn. Our art pieces may be exhibited at the fair too. The teacher or us may put decorative pottery or sculptures on display. Visitors to the art fair get a chance to see the very best work we can do. Future world-famous artists might be us.

B. Using Pronouns in Writing

Imagine that your school is putting on an art fair with different booths where you can try your hand at different arts and crafts. Write a paragraph about the artists, parents, teachers, and students who attend. Be sure to use subject pronouns correctly.

_____

_____

_____

_____

_____

_____

_____

_____

_____

_____

_____

Copyright © McDougal Littell/Houghton Mifflin Company.

CHAPTER 3

Lesson 3

Object Pronouns

Teaching

Object pronouns are personal pronouns used as direct objects, as indirect objects, or as the objects of prepositions.

Object Pronouns	
Singular	**Plural**
me	us
you	you
him, her, it	them

As a **direct object,** the pronoun receives the action of a verb and answers the question *whom* or *what*. As an **indirect object,** the pronoun tells *to whom or what* or *for whom or what* an action is performed. As an **object of a preposition,** the pronoun follows a preposition such as *to, from, for, against, by, between,* or *about*.

Direct object	Matt bought the camera on <u>display</u>. (*What* did he buy? *camera*)
Indirect object	He loaned <u>me</u> the camera. (*To whom* did he loan? *me*)
Object of the preposition	I borrowed the camera from <u>him</u> several times.

A. Identifying Object Pronouns

Underline all the object pronouns in the following sentences.

1. Matt's family is very large, and he takes many pictures of them.
2. He gives them pictures for their photo albums.
3. I suggested to him that he might enjoy taking pictures of famous buildings around town too.
4. When he visited downtown, he gave it a try.
5. Later he showed me some pictures of the buildings he had shot.
6. I liked them and so did the judges at a local contest where Matt won first prize.

B. Using Object Pronouns

Underline the correct pronoun to complete each sentence.

1. Mariah's parents built a photography lab for (she, her) in the basement.
2. They bought (her, she) film, paper, and photography chemicals.
3. Mariah thanked (them, they) once she saw what they had done.
4. She had a roll of film and wanted to develop (them, it) right away.
5. Mariah's parents were impressed when she showed (they, them) her pictures.
6. No one taught (her, she) the rules for developing pictures.
7. She learned (they, them) by herself.

Copyright © McDougal Littell/Houghton Mifflin Company.

CHAPTER 3

Lesson 3 Object Pronouns

A. Using Object Pronouns

In each sentence, underline the pronoun that completes each sentence correctly.

1. "We bought (she, her) a doll for her fourth birthday," said Taylor's parents.

2. Her mother explains, "She has begged (us, we) for a doll on every birthday since that day."

3. Would you believe (I, me) if I told you she has over 40 dolls now?

4. All her relatives give (her, she) dolls for her birthdays.

5. Because her dolls are collectibles, she has never played with (them, they).

6. She has a younger brother, and she has given (he, him) strict rules about handling her precious dolls.

7. Sometimes she places (them, they) on high shelves that are out of his reach.

8. Between you and (I, me), I know that two of her dolls are worth about $500 each.

9. Taylor has shown (me, I) her favorite doll, the one she got for her sixth birthday.

10. I agreed that it was a beautiful doll, but I told (her, she) I liked another one better.

11. Taylor loves her dolls; sometimes it seems she likes (they, them) more than she likes her human friends.

12. Taylor says that the best gift anyone could ever give (her, she) is another beautiful doll.

B. Choosing Object Pronouns

Fill in the blanks in the following sentences with appropriate object pronouns. Vary the pronouns you use, and do not use the pronoun *you*.

1. The elves hid in the woods, where nobody could find _____.

2. A huge bear growled at Marilee, then ran away from _____.

3. The teacher told _____ where we should sit in the auditorium.

4. The matador fanned his cape, and the bull charged toward _____.

5. After Al and I entered a password, the computer spoke to _____.

6. Ceres searched for her lovely daughter but couldn't find _____.

7. I gave the robot an order, and it followed _____ around the room.

8. When the kindergartners sat on the carpet, their teacher read a picture book to

_____

Copyright © McDougal Littell/Houghton Mifflin Company.

Lesson 3 · Object Pronouns   *Application*

A. Proofreading

The following story contains several errors in the use of object pronouns. When you find a pronoun used incorrectly, cross it out. Then insert this proofreading symbol ⌄ and write the correct pronoun above it.

Magicians have been performing tricks for thousands of years. Amazingly, magic still entertains us. Most magicians start performing magic as children. For example, my younger brother Scott likes magic. I gave he a book on magic a few years ago. His classmates like magic, so he tries new tricks for they. He is truly a master of deception. He has explained some tricks to I, and I still cannot see how he does them. He has even invented some tricks of his own. In one of his newest tricks, he uses our pet bird, Molly. He makes her disappear and then reappear. He spends hours every day perfecting his tricks. He doesn't like anyone to bother he when he is at work. If he keeps trying, perhaps he will someday join the ranks of the great magicians.

B. Using Object Pronouns in Writing

What is your hobby? Do you like computers? Do you trade baseball cards? Are you an enthusiastic reader? Do you like to take photographs? Write about a time when you pursued your hobby, for example, a time when you added to your collection or worked on a special project. Use at least four object pronouns in your paragraph.

_____

_____

_____

_____

_____

_____

_____

_____

_____

_____

_____

Copyright © McDougal Littell/Houghton Mifflin Company.

Lesson 4 Possessive Pronouns

Teaching

Possessive pronouns are personal pronouns used to show ownership or relationship.

Possessive Pronouns	
Singular	**Plural**
my, mine	our, ours
your, yours	your, yours
her, hers, his, its	their, theirs

The possessive pronouns *my, your, her, his, our,* and *their* come before nouns. The possessive pronouns *mine, ours, yours, his, hers,* and *theirs* can stand alone in a sentence.

> <u>My</u> mother is a great painter.
> Some people's talents are in sports. <u>Mine</u> is in music.

Some possessive pronouns sound like contractions (*its/it's, your/you're, their/they're*). Don't confuse these pairs. Remember that possessive pronouns never use apostrophes. Contractions *always* use apostrophes.

Contraction <u>It's</u> my goal to play professional basketball.
Possessive Why did that team succeed? <u>Its</u> secret was practice.

A. Identifying Possessive Pronouns

Underline all the possessive pronouns in the following sentences.

1. All of us have our special talents and abilities.
2. For example, Mozart was a musical genius. His father had him perform as a child before the kings of Europe.
3. Mozart's musical talent was great, but what is your special ability?
4. Because of a combination of natural talent and hard work, his was a future filled with promise.
5. Your gift may be an ability to inspire people with your words; mine might be the way I draw or paint.

B. Using Possessive Pronouns

Underline the correct word to complete each sentence.

1. Winston Churchill was a great leader, and (his, its) speeches encouraged the citizens of Great Britain during the war.
2. The English people were discouraged because (they're, their) country was suffering terrible disasters.
3. Churchill's words showed England that (it's, its) future was in the hands of the English.
4. You never know when (your, you're) special gift will prove useful.
5. (Your, You're) talents may be hidden now, but you should try to develop them.

Copyright © McDougal Littell/Houghton Mifflin Company.

Name _____ Date _____

Possessive Pronouns

More Practice

A. Using Possessive Pronouns

In each sentence, underline the word that completes each sentence correctly.

1. I share (my, mine) talent for making people laugh with everyone I meet.
2. Some professional athletes want the fame without (its, it's) responsibility.
3. Martha Graham was a leader in modern dance. (Her, Hers) dances were beautiful.
4. (Your, You're) field hockey team is talented but not very dedicated.
5. Our Olympic swimmers are improving, but (their, theirs) are the best in the world.
6. Emily Dickinson wrote poems with deeply personal meanings, but not many people knew of (her, hers) talent during her lifetime.
7. When will (your, you're) special talent become clear to you?
8. Many talented young musicians dream of seeing (their, they're) videos on TV.
9. No matter what (it's, its) cost, you should pursue your goal.
10. If we don't use (our, ours) talents, we may lose them.

B. Choosing Possessive Pronouns

Fill in the blanks in the following sentences with the appropriate possessive pronoun. Vary the pronouns you use.

1. Monkeys take good care of _____ young.

2. Is _____ baby sister awake now?

3. _____ ears are bombarded by all sorts of noises all day.

4. What are _____ views on using animals in scientific experiments?

5. Your dog is bigger than _____.

6. Our car is older than _____.

7. The woodpecker uses _____ sharp beak like a chisel.

8. Some people lose _____ hearing because of loud noises.

9. Today's weather is depressing me with _____ gray skies and cold winds.

10. If you can guess the winning number, the prize is _____.

Copyright © McDougal Littell/Houghton Mifflin Company.

Lesson 4 Possessive Pronouns   *Application*

A. Proofreading

Proofread the following story to make sure that possessive pronouns have been
used in the right places. When you find a pronoun used incorrectly, cross it out.
Then insert this proofreading symbol ⌃ and write the correct pronoun above it.

    Everyone has different talents. We just have to discover our. Sometimes,

talents are found in ways that you don't expect. That's why it's important to

try different things. You're fear of failure may stop you from finding a hidden

talent. Its not smart to let that happen. Instead, you should try your hand at

doing new things. Some of our most talented musicians started when their

parents made them take music lessons. By playing music, they discovered it's

beauty. You can also develop more than one talent. Mine best talent was in

writing, but I also learned to be an expert ski instructor. So take some time to

think of your interests and the many things to do in this world. You may find

you're unexplored talents are waiting for you.

B. Using Possessive Pronouns in Writing

What talents or gifts make you special? Write a paragraph about your gifts. Use at
least five possessive pronouns in your paragraph.

_____

_____

_____

_____

_____

_____

_____

_____

_____

_____

_____

Copyright © McDougal Littell/Houghton Mifflin Company.

CHAPTER 3

Lesson 5

Reflexive and Intensive Pronouns

Teaching

Pronouns that end in *-self* or *-selves* are either **reflexive** or **intensive** pronouns.

Reflexive and Intensive Pronouns		
myself	yourself	herself, himself, itself
ourselves	yourselves	themselves

A **reflexive pronoun** refers to the subject and directs the action of the verb back to the subject. Reflexive pronouns are necessary to the meaning of a sentence. Without them the sentence doesn't make sense.

> The emperor convinced <u>himself</u> that the cloth was beautiful.
> ("The emperor convinced that the cloth was beautiful" doesn't make sense.)

An **intensive pronoun** emphasizes the noun or pronoun within the same sentence. Intensive pronouns are not necessary to the meaning of the sentence.

> I <u>myself</u> would have laughed at the sight.
> ("I would have laughed at the sight" still makes sense without the word *myself*.)

Remember that *hisself* and *theirselves* are not real words. Never use them. Use *himself* and *themselves* instead.

A. Identifying Reflexive and Intensive Pronouns

Underline all the reflexive and intensive pronouns in the following sentences.

1. When I feel discouraged, I tell myself the story of the ugly duckling.

2. The other ducklings played games by themselves and ignored the ugly duckling.

3. The ugly duckling himself could not understand why no one liked him.

4. Because he was different, the ducklings saw themselves as better than him.

5. The ugly duckling thought, I need to hide myself far away from the others.

6. After the winter, the ugly duckling caught a glimpse of himself in the water.

7. He saw himself for what he really was—a beautiful swan.

B. Using Reflexive and Intensive Pronouns

Underline the correct pronoun to complete each sentence.

1. The emperor (him, himself) was a vain man.

2. Two tailors told (themselves, theirselves) that they could fool the emperor.

3. They said that the emperor's robe would make (itself, it) visible only to the smartest people.

4. None of us wanted to prove (us, ourselves) stupid by saying we couldn't see it.

5. Finally a little boy laughed and shouted, "The emperor should look at (him, himself). He isn't wearing anything at all!"

Copyright © McDougal Littell/Houghton Mifflin Company.

CHAPTER 3

Lesson 5

Reflexive and Intensive Pronouns

More Practice

A. Using Reflexive and Intensive Pronouns

In each sentence, decide if the boldfaced pronoun is reflexive or intensive. Write **R** for reflexive and **I** for intensive on the line.

1. People have been telling **themselves** the story of Snow White for centuries. _____

2. The queen knew that she **herself** was not as beautiful as Snow White. _____

3. The queen talked **herself** into getting rid of Snow White. _____

4. She told one of her men to kill Snow White, but the hunter **himself** knew he could not do it. _____

5. He told Snow White, "Save **yourself**! Never return to the castle." _____

6. Snow White ran for a long time and eventually found **herself** at a small cottage. _____

7. The owners **themselves** said they were the Seven Dwarves. _____

8. Snow White busied **herself** with cleaning and cooking for the kind little men. _____

9. Later, the queen **herself** set out to make sure that Snow White would die. _____

10. The queen disguised **herself** as a poor old woman and gave Snow White a poisoned apple. _____

11. I'm sure that you **yourself** can finish this story. (Remember? A prince kisses Snow White, and she wakes up and marries him, and they live happily ever after.) _____

B. Choosing Reflexive and Intensive Pronouns

Fill in the blanks in the following sentences with the appropriate reflexive or intensive pronoun. On the line to the right, write **R** for reflexive or **I** for intensive.

1. The students _____ will make their views known. _____

2. The mayor introduced _____ to as many voters as she could. _____

3. The wheel rim _____ may need to be replaced. _____

4. We hope he will not blame _____ for the mistake. _____

5. I know _____ well enough to stay away from the candy store. _____

6. You _____ could be your own worst enemy. _____

Copyright © McDougal Littell/Houghton Mifflin Company.

Lesson 5

Reflexive and Intensive Pronouns

Application

A. Proofreading

Proofread the following story to make sure that reflexive and intensive pronouns have been used correctly. When you find a pronoun used incorrectly, cross it out. Then insert this proofreading symbol ⌃ and write the correct pronoun above it.

Three pig brothers were growing up fast. They told theirselves that it was time to go out on their own. The first little pig quickly built a straw house for hisself. It was a fine house, but unfortunately the pigs' enemy—the big bad wolf—blew it down easily. The second little pig built him a house of twigs. This pig told hisself that he would be safe in his flimsy twig house. However, again the big bad wolf huffed and puffed, and the twig house fell down. The two little pigs ran over to the third pig's house. This pig hisself was not worried about the big bad wolf because his house was built of strong bricks. Later, the wolf thought to himself that he could blow the brick house down. But you and I both know that his huffing and puffing was worthless against the strength of bricks. You should tell you this story when you are tempted to take the easy way out of a problem. Remember that the easy way is not always the best way.

B. Using Reflexive and Intensive Pronouns in Writing

Retell a simple fairy tale or folktale on the lines below. Use at least four reflexive or intensive pronouns in your story.

_____

_____

_____

_____

_____

_____

_____

_____

_____

_____

Copyright © McDougal Littell/Houghton Mifflin Company.

Lesson 6 · Interrogatives and Demonstratives   *Teaching*

An **interrogative pronoun** is used to introduce a question. Interrogative pronouns include *who, whom, what, which,* and *whose.*

Who is always used as a subject or a predicate pronoun.

Subject	<u>Who</u> created this dance?
Predicate pronoun	The dancer was <u>who</u>?

Whom is always used as an object.

Direct object	<u>Whom</u> do you choose for your partner?
Indirect object	Paula taught <u>whom</u> the new dance step?
Object of preposition	With <u>whom</u> will I dance next?

Don't confuse *whose* with *who's. Who* is a contraction that means *who is* or *who has.*

<u>Who's</u> ready for some ice cream?
<u>Whose</u> is the car parked in front of the house?

A **demonstrative pronoun** points out a person, place, thing, or idea. The demonstrative pronouns—*this, that, these,* and *those*—are used alone in a sentence. Never use *here* or *there* with a demonstrative pronoun.

Singular	<u>This</u> is my bedroom. <u>That</u> is my computer.
Plural	<u>These</u> are my tickets. <u>Those</u> are yours.

A. Using Interrogative Pronouns
Underline the pronoun that correctly completes each sentence.

1. (Who, Whom) won the championship last year?
2. By (who, whom) was that poem written?
3. (Who, Whom) did the president appoint as secretary of defense?
4. To (who, whom) did you give an invitation?
5. (Whose, Who's) are these books on the kitchen table?
6. (Who, Whom) was the first human to reach the South Pole?
7. You gave (who, whom) the combination to the safe?
8. (Who, Whom) makes the best apple strudel?

B. Using Demonstrative Pronouns
Underline the correct pronoun to complete each sentence.

1. (That, Those) are the cherries that taste sweetest.
2. (Those, That) is the dog that howls all night.
3. (This here, This) is the house where I live.
4. (That, That there) was the only idea I could come up with.
5. (These here, These) were the only coats left in the closet.
6. (This, These) is the most expensive necklace I own.

Copyright © McDougal Littell/Houghton Mifflin Company.

Lesson 6 # Interrogatives and Demonstratives   *More Practice*

A. Using Interrogative Pronouns

Write *who*, *whom*, or *whose* on the line to complete the following sentences.

1. _____ is willing to wash the windows today?

2. _____ are you ordering around?

3. _____ did the general salute as he walked by?

4. With _____ are we going to the concert?

5. _____ are these old sneakers?

6. _____ is ready with his or her report today?

7. The author is _____?

8. To _____ will the server give the check?

9. _____ is this autographed picture of Mickey Mantle?

10. You gave _____ the map to the treasure?

B. Choosing Demonstrative Pronouns

Write a demonstrative pronoun on the line in each sentence.

1. _____ is the school my brother attends.

2. _____ are the photographs from my summer vacation.

3. We were looking for a quilt, but we found _____ instead.

4. If you want help with _____, just let us know.

5. If I had known _____, I wouldn't have called you.

6. _____ are the reasons for my decision.

7. _____ makes me wonder if I did the right thing.

8. _____ were the books I used for my report.

9. Mr. Gale is looking for bushes for his garden, but _____ need too much sun.

10. Some malls are boring, but _____ one has some new and different stores.

Copyright © McDougal Littell/Houghton Mifflin Company.

CHAPTER 3

Lesson 6 — Interrogatives and Demonstratives *Application*

A. Writing Sentences with Interrogative Pronouns

Write a question that you could use in the following situations. Be sure to follow the instructions in parentheses after each situation description.

1. You want to know the name of the person who stars in a movie. (Use *who.*)

_____

2. You want to know the name of the person who directed the movie. (Use *whom.*)

_____

3. You want to find out if anyone will come to the movie with you. (Use *who.*)

_____

4. You want to find out the name of the actor who won an award. (Use *whom.*)

_____

5. You want to find out who wrote the script. (Use *who* or *whom.*)

_____

B. Using Pronouns in Writing

Imagine that you have come in late to a television mystery your sister was watching. You are not sure what is happening and who did what. Write five questions you would ask your sister during the commercial. Use the interrogative pronouns *who, whom* and *whose.*

1. _____

_____

2. _____

_____

3. _____

_____

4. _____

_____

5. _____

_____

Copyright © McDougal Littell/Houghton Mifflin Company.

CHAPTER 3

Lesson 7

Pronoun-Antecedent Agreement   *Teaching*

The **antecedent** is the noun or pronoun that a pronoun refers to or replaces. Pronouns must agree with their antecedents in number, person, and gender.

Number Use a singular pronoun to refer to a singular antecedent. Use a plural pronoun to refer to a plural antecedent.

> <u>America</u>, with <u>its</u> great opportunities, was attractive to immigrants.

> <u>Immigrants</u> came to America. <u>They</u> were looking for a better way of life.

Person The **person** (first person, second person, third person) of a pronoun must be the same as the person of the antecedent. Avoid switching from one person to another in the same sentence or paragraph.

First Person	<u>We</u> learned about <u>our</u> ancestors.
Second Person	<u>You</u> can learn about <u>your</u> ancestors too.
Third Person	<u>Luis</u> knows that <u>his</u> ancestors came from Spain.

Gender The **gender** of a pronoun must be the same as the gender of its antecedent. Personal pronouns have three gender forms: masculine *(he, him, his)*, feminine *(she, her, hers)*, and neuter *(it, its)*. Don't use only masculine or feminine pronouns when you mean to refer to both genders.

> <u>Mrs. Kim</u> writes to <u>her</u> relatives in Korea.
> <u>Jacob</u> knows stories from <u>his</u> family's homeland.
> An <u>immigrant</u> leaves <u>his</u> or <u>her</u> homeland.

Identifying Pronouns and Their Antecedents

In each sentence underline the personal pronoun once and its antecedent twice.

1. Because it has received many immigrants, the United States has been called a nation of immigrants.
2. Many immigrants came to America hoping they would become rich.
3. Many immigrants left their homelands for religious freedom.
4. Alexander Graham Bell was an immigrant from Scotland. He invented the telephone.
5. When Frank's great-grandfather came to Ellis Island, officials there misspelled his name.
6. Enrique is proud of his Spanish heritage.
7. Marie is researching her Polish family's history.
8. Bridget told the class, "My parents came from Ireland."
9. Lenore is using the computer to track her family's history.
10. Do you know any customs of your ancestors?
11. We should be proud of our ancestors' accomplishments.

Copyright © McDougal Littell/Houghton Mifflin Company.

Lesson 7

Pronoun-Antecedent Agreement

More Practice

A. Identifying Pronouns and Their Antecedents

In each sentence draw an arrow to connect each pronoun with its antecedent.

1. We will share foods and customs at our multicultural fair.

2. Anthony will bring a dish of his family's spaghetti and meatballs.

3. Clare will show some coins that her grandparents brought from Greece.

4. I will share my great-grandmother's old photographs from China.

5. We marked on a map the countries from which our ancestors came.

6. When immigrants arrived from around the world, they brought many different customs.

7. Because the United States has so many immigrants, its culture is rich and varied.

8. Sometimes U.S. citizens need to be tolerant of new immigrants and their ways.

9. I am proud of the way my family always stressed the importance of education.

10. You should bring some of your family photographs to share with others at the fair.

B. Making Pronouns and Antecedents Agree

On the line write a pronoun that correctly completes each sentence. Also underline the antecedent of the pronoun.

1. Since ancient times, children have worked to help _____ families.

2. Sally Ride made history when _____ became the first U.S. woman in space.

3. The sharp quills on the porcupine protect _____ from predators.

4. Paul Bunyan, a giant lumberjack, combed _____ beard with a pine tree.

5. Margaret wrote about _____ experiences in a diary.

6. After the spaceship was launched, _____ circled the earth.

7. King Arthur and _____ knights arrived at the beautiful city of Camelot.

8. Bats hang upside down when _____ are sleeping.

9. The baseball players should wash _____ uniforms this weekend.

10. The girl was funny. _____ made us all laugh.

Copyright © McDougal Littell/Houghton Mifflin Company.

Pronoun-Antecedent Agreement

Application

A. Making Pronouns and Antecedents Agree in Writing

Read the following paragraph. Look especially for errors in agreement between pronouns and their antecedents. On the lines below, write the numbers of the sentences with agreement errors. Then write each of those sentences correctly.

(1) The first sight of America for many immigrants was the Statue of Liberty; they became a symbol of freedom. (2) As the immigrants passed the statue, they studied it with awe, realizing that they were finally in the United States. (3) Many immigrants spent his first few hours in America at Ellis Island. (4) The government had opened a reception center for them on the island in 1892. (5) There, doctors examined it for illnesses. (6) If an immigrant was judged to be unhealthy, it or she might be sent back home. (7) Many immigrants stayed in New York because she had spent all its money just to reach America. (8) The immigrants had heard that the U.S. was the land of opportunity and freedom. (9) For most, they became the land of hard work. (10) Ellis Island is now open to the public, and he has become a popular destination for tourists.

_____

_____

_____

_____

_____

_____

_____

_____

_____

_____

_____

_____

_____

B. Writing with Pronouns

Imagine that you are an immigrant coming to the U.S. today. What sights strike you as most interesting? What kinds of people do you see? What are you feeling? On a separate sheet of paper, write a journal entry about your experiences. Be sure to include at least four personal pronouns with clear antecedents.

Copyright © McDougal Littell/Houghton Mifflin Company.

CHAPTER 3

CHAPTER 3

Lesson 8 # Indefinite Pronoun Agreement *Teaching*

An **indefinite pronoun** does not refer to a specific person, place, thing, or idea. Indefinite pronouns often do not have antecedents.

Indefinite pronouns can be singular, plural, or singular or plural.

Indefinite Pronouns					
Singular				**Plural**	**Singular or Plural**
another	each	everything	one	both	all none
anybody	either	neither	somebody	few	any some
anyone	everybody	nobody	someone	many	most
anything	everyone	no one	something	several	

Use a singular pronoun to refer to a singular indefinite pronoun. Use *his or her* when the antecedent could be either masculine or feminine.

> Everyone made his or her own costume.

Use a plural personal pronoun to refer to a plural indefinite pronoun.

> Several designed their costumes. (plural)

Some indefinite pronouns can be singular or plural. Often, the phrase that follows the indefinite pronoun tells you whether the indefinite pronoun is singular or plural.

> All of the excitement had reached its peak. (singular)

> All of the audience members took their seats. (plural)

Using Indefinite Pronouns

In each sentence, underline the correct pronoun.

1. All of the students at Edison Middle School can tell you (his or her, their) major reason for enjoying March.

2. That is the month many of the classes put on (its, their) own plays.

3. Each of the classes chooses the play (they, it) will put on.

4. Most of the students prefer acting as (his or her, their) best job.

5. Some choose (his or her, their) roles as crew members.

6. In Ms. Weil's class, everybody was happy with (his or her, their) part to play.

7. None of the students forgot (his or her, their) lines at dress rehearsal.

8. On the day of the play, one of the lead actors lost (their, her) voice.

9. How could anyone say lines without (his or her, their) voice?

10. Luckily, by the time the play began, everyone had recovered (their, his or her) health.

11. All of the actors acted (his or her, their) parts with energy.

12. The students had a great time; in fact, many look back on the March play as one of (his or her, their) favorite school experiences.

Copyright © McDougal Littell/Houghton Mifflin Company.

Lesson 8 Indefinite Pronoun Agreement   *More Practice*

A. Identifying indefinite Pronouns

Underline the indefinite pronoun in each sentence. Then underline the correct pronoun in parentheses.

1. Many of the early explorers risked (his or her, their) lives to discover new worlds.
2. Everybody can do (his or her, their) part in caring for the environment.
3. A few of the astronauts spent (his or her, their) time in the space station.
4. Everyone wrote a letter expressing (his or her, their) concern over the pollution in the lake.
5. Either of the contestants has (his or her, their) chance to win a trip to Toronto.
6. Both of the storytellers told (his or her, their) versions of how the world began.
7. Each of the scuba divers wore (his or her, their) face mask and snorkel.
8. One of the pitchers signed (her, their) name on my baseball.
9. Several of the skydivers jumped from the plane, opened (his or her, their) parachutes, and floated safely to the ground.
10. Neither of the knights lost (his, their) courage during the battle.
11. Some of the molasses is stuck to the sides of (its, their) bottle.
12. If any of our guests need a ride to the airport, tell (him or her, them) to call a taxi.

B. Using Pronouns Correctly

In each sentence below, decide whether the pronouns agree with their antecedents. If the sentence is correct, write **Correct** on the line. If it contains a pronoun that does not agree with its antecedent, rewrite the sentence correctly on the line.

1. Everyone had practiced their lines for several weeks.

   _____

2. All of the teachers were proud of their classes.

   _____

3. Some of the parents helped his or her children memorize lines.

   _____

4. Several took time off from his or her jobs to see the play.

   _____

Copyright © McDougal Littell/Houghton Mifflin Company.

Lesson 8 · Indefinite Pronoun Agreement — *Application*

A. Proofreading for Indefinite Pronoun Agreement

Proofread the following paragraph. When you find a pronoun-antecedent error, cross the pronoun out. Then insert this proofreading symbol ∧ and write the correct pronoun or pronouns above it. If necessary, mark any verb that must agree with the changed pronoun to be changed, also.

All of the students in Ms. Miller's and Mr. Tompkins's classes were picking out his or her favorite plays. Each was asked to give his or her reasons for choosing that play. A few of the girls selected *The Blue Umbrella* as her favorite because she felt close to its main character. Some of the boys chose *The Dangerous Summer* because they liked the excitement and suspense of that play. Somebody else said that they liked only funny plays with happy endings like *The Good Years.* Both of the teachers had a hard time selecting his or her favorite plays. Ms. Miller finally chose *Sleeping Beauty* because she has always loved that story. Did any of the students choose the same play as Ms. Miller? Surprisingly, no one else chose *Sleeping Beauty* as their favorite play, but many chose Mr. Tompkins's favorite, *The Looking Glass,* because he or she liked mysteries.

B. Using Indefinite Pronouns in Writing

Write a paragraph about a class project you have taken part in. Explain what your role was in the project and tell what other people did. Use at least four indefinite pronouns. Be sure that any personal pronouns agree with their indefinite pronoun antecedents in number.

_____

_____

_____

_____

_____

_____

_____

_____

Copyright © McDougal Littell/Houghton Mifflin Company.

Copyright © McDougal Littell/Houghton Mifflin Company.

Lesson 9

Pronoun Problems

Teaching

We and *Us* with Nouns

The pronouns *we* and *us* are sometimes followed by a noun that identifies the pronoun (*we neighbors, us neighbors*).

Use *we* when the noun is a subject or a predicate noun. Use *us* when the noun is an object.

> <u>We</u> neighbors had a block party. (*We* had a block party.)
> The firefighters gave <u>us</u> neighbors a peek inside the fire engine.
> (They gave *us* a peek inside the fire engine.)

Unclear Reference

Be sure that each personal pronoun refers clearly to only one person, place, or thing. If your reader will be confused, use a noun instead of a pronoun.

> **Confusing** Don and Zak like to go to the beach, but he can't swim very well.
> (*Who* can't swim well?)
>
> **Clear** Don and Zak like to go to the beach, but Zak can't swim very well.

A. Choosing the Correct Pronoun

In each sentence, underline the correct pronoun form.

1. (We, Us) diners waited a long time for our food.
2. The director gave (we, us) actors new lines to learn.
3. (We, Us) hockey players must come early to get time on the ice.
4. The movie star sent autographed pictures of herself to (we, us) fans.
5. The guide showed (we, us) visitors the museum's latest find.
6. Mules took (us, we) tourists to the bottom of Grand Canyon.
7. The most dissatisfied citizens were (we, us) residents of the Tremont neighborhood.
8. If (we, us) volunteers work together, we can make a difference.

B. Avoiding Unclear Reference

In each set, circle the letter of the sentence that is stated more clearly.

1. a. Aunt Gina and Mom are both good cooks, but she doesn't like her cooking.
   b. Aunt Gina and Mom are both good cooks, but Mom doesn't like Aunt Gina's cooking.
2. a. When the king and the prince sit at a table, the prince sits on the king's right.
   b. When the king and the prince sit at a table, he sits on his right.
3. a. Gary and Ed worked on the project, but he did most of the work.
   b. Gary and Ed worked on the project, but Ed did most of the work.

CHAPTER 3

Lesson 9 Pronoun Problems   *More Practice*

A. Choosing the Correct Pronoun

In each sentence, underline the correct pronoun form.

1. The leader gave (we, us) scouts our certificates.
2. Should (we, us) swimmers report for practice today?
3. The contestants in the quiz show sat with (we, us) audience members.
4. (We, Us) players are going to the championship game.
5. Most of (we, us) club members will help in the volunteer project.
6. No one told (we, us) cheerleaders about the time for the pep rally.
7. Whenever (we, us) cousins get together, we play board games.
8. The most surprised contestants were (we, us) winners.
9. For (we, us) scientists, the discovery of a new planet would be exciting.
10. Although (we, us) shoppers came early, the store was all out of the latest toy craze by the time we got there.

B. Avoiding Unclear Reference

Rewrite each of these sentences to make them clear, not confusing.

1. Terry and Inez both wrote essays about the topic, but I liked hers better.

   _____

2. The doctor and the nurse discussed the patient, but she didn't make herself clear.

   _____

3. Michael and Antoine did research on the Internet, and he found a great site.

   _____

4. Bob and Dan were playing catch when he was suddenly called home for dinner.

   _____

5. The train and the bus left Milwaukee at the same time, but it arrived in Chicago first.

   _____

6. Dana and Michelle both like dogs, and she helps her walk dogs as a part-time job.

   _____

Copyright © McDougal Littell/Houghton Mifflin Company.

CHAPTER 3

Lesson 9 · Pronoun Problems   *Application*

A. Using Pronouns Correctly

Use each of the phrases printed below in an original sentence.

> **EXAMPLE** we runners
> *We runners worked to improve our times.*

1. us passengers _____

_____

2. we dancers _____

_____

3. us hikers _____

_____

4. we players _____

_____

B. Proofreading for Correct Pronoun Usage

The following paragraph is filled with unclear references. Rewrite the paragraph
more clearly on the lines below.

> Hector and Raymond were walking through the woods one day when
> he saw what looked like a cave opening. He knelt down and saw that the
> opening was large enough to crawl through. After he crawled into the cave, he
> called for Raymond to come, too. He followed, and they both were amazed at
> how dark the cave was. He got nervous and told him that they shouldn't go
> any further into the cave until they got flashlights. They both crawled out of
> the cave and then went to his home where they picked up
> a flashlight. When they came back to the forest, they searched all over but
> could never find the cave again.

_____

_____

_____

_____

_____

_____

_____

Copyright © McDougal Littell/Houghton Mifflin Company.

CHAPTER 3

Lesson 10 # More Pronoun Problems   *Teaching*

Using Pronouns in Compounds Use the subject pronouns *I, she, he, we,* and *they* in a compound subject or a compound predicate pronoun. Use the object pronouns *me, her, him, us,* and *them* in a compound object.

Compound subject	<u>Bonnie and he</u> were bank robbers.
Compound predicate pronoun	Wanted criminals were <u>Clyde and she</u>.
Compound object	Law officers chased <u>Clyde and her</u>.

Phrases That Interfere Sometimes words and phrases come between a subject and a pronoun that refers to it. Be sure the pronoun agrees with the subject.

These <u>criminals</u>, like other desperate people during the Depression, risked <u>their</u> lives for money. (*Their* refers to *criminals*.)

A. Using Pronouns in Compounds

Underline the pronoun that completes each sentence correctly.

1. Bonnie Parker met Clyde Barrow in 1932. Clyde and (her, she) became famous criminals.
2. Bonnie and (he, she) liked to steal cars and rob banks.
3. Once, Clyde landed in jail, but Bonnie handed him a gun during a visit. After he broke out of jail, the police were after Bonnie and (he, him) again.
4. One day, (him, he) and Bonnie took pictures of each other with machine guns.
5. The harm they were doing seemed to mean nothing to Clyde and (her, she).
6. Together, Clyde and (she, her) killed a dozen innocent people.
7. Fugitives from the law were (them, they).
8. One day, Clyde and (she, her) got in a terrible car accident.
9. They found a place where Bonnie and (him, he) could get better.

B. Dealing with Phrases That Interfere

Draw arrows from the boldfaced pronouns to the words they modify.

1. Clyde, who had committed most of the crimes, hoped **his** health would return.
2. Months later, these fugitives from the law went back to **their** illegal ways.
3. On the day they died, the couple had **their** car stopped by police.
4. After the gunfire ended, Bonnie was found with a machine gun across **her** lap.

Copyright © McDougal Littell/Houghton Mifflin Company.

CHAPTER 3

Lesson 10

More Pronoun Problems

More Practice

A. Using Pronouns in Compounds

Underline the pronoun that completes each sentence correctly.

1. Neil Armstrong and (he, him) planted a U.S. flag on the moon.

2. Clarence and (I, me) drew a map of an imaginary island.

3. Ben described the powwow in Arizona to Victor and (she, her).

4. The ones who defeated the scary monster were Galahad and (them, they).

5. Sylvia invited you and (I, me) to the jazz festival in the park.

6. Tina and (she, her) saw an exhibit about garbage at the children's museum.

7. The judges awarded first prize to Michelle and (he, him).

8. My teacher told the others and (I, me) about the adventures of Sinbad the Sailor.

9. The ballerinas featured in the show were Bernice and (she, her).

10. The boys across the street threw snowballs at Tom and (him, he).

B. Dealing with Phrases That Interfere

Decide if the pronouns in each sentence are used correctly. If the sentence has an error, rewrite it on the line. If the sentence is written correctly, write **Correct** on the line.

1. Clyde, though wanted for many crimes, continued their robberies.

_____

_____

2. Bonnie often wrote poems about their life with Clyde.

_____

_____

3. These fugitives had its pictures in post offices all over the country.

_____

_____

4. Their car, after the final shootout, had bullet holes all over its doors and windows.

_____

_____

5. The relatives of the criminal were ashamed of its famous family member.

_____

_____

6. Bonnie, like many other criminals, came to their end in a violent way.

_____

_____

Copyright © McDougal Littell/Houghton Mifflin Company.

Lesson 10

More Pronoun Problems

Application

A. Proofreading

Proofread this paragraph. Look especially for errors in the use of pronouns. When you find an error, cross out the pronoun used incorrectly. Insert this symbol ∧ and write the correct pronoun above it.

Bonnie and Clyde were not people you would choose to be your friends. When Bonnie met Clyde, he was a petty thief with big plans. Bonnie and him felt a bond because both of them loved excitement. A big night for Clyde and her was robbing a store and making a clean getaway. Bonnie thought their life was romantic and even wrote poems about herself and he. But Bonnie hadn't counted on murdering anyone. After Clyde killed a man, him and Bonnie were forced to live life on the run. An unheated car was home for Bonnie and he for months at a time. The excitement of the crime wore off as police chased Clyde and she over several states during the 1930s. Because of Bonnie and him, 12 people lost their lives. So, it wasn't surprising that police were determined to find the couple. After two years of running, Clyde and her were finally killed in a shootout in Louisiana.

B. Making Pronouns Agree with Their Antecedents

Below are the beginnings of several sentences. Each beginning contains the sentence's subject. For each sentence beginning, choose an ending from the list below. Write your ending on the line.

EXAMPLE The sheriff with his deputies listened to *his radio*.

his brother's gang	her daughter's poor health
their toughness	his shotgun
his cash register	

1. Clyde with a group of desperate friends picked up _____.

2. The shopkeeper in the little store nervously opened _____.

3. Bonnie's mother, during a visit, was surprised when she saw _____

_____.

4. Buck, Clyde's brother, joined _____.

5. The criminals, whose crimes were reported in the newspaper, became well known for

_____.

Copyright © McDougal Littell/Houghton Mifflin Company.

Lesson 1

What Is a Verb?

Teaching

A **verb** is a word used to express an action, a condition, or a state of being. The two main kinds of verbs are action verbs and linking verbs. Both kinds can be accompanied by helping verbs.

An **action verb** tells what the subject does. The action may be physical or mental.

> The fish <u>swims</u> in water. (physical action)   I <u>believe</u> in unicorns. (mental action)

A **linking verb** links the subject of the sentence to a word in the predicate. The most common linking verbs are forms of the verb *be*.

Linking Verbs Sample verbs	
Forms of *be*	be, is, am, are, was, were, been, being
Verbs that express condition	appear, become, feel, grow, look, seem, smell, sound, remain, taste

Some verbs may serve as either action verbs or as linking verbs.

> The rabbit **appeared** from the bush. (action)   It **appeared** frightened. (linking)

Helping verbs help the main verb express action or show time. They are combined with the main verbs to form **verb phrases.**

> The bear **has run** away. (The helping verb is *has*. The main verb is *run*.)

A few verbs can serve as either helping verbs or main verbs.

> That bear **has** a baby cub. (The main verb is *has*.)

Common Helping Verbs	
Forms of *have:* has, have, had	Forms of *be:* be, am, is, are, was, were, been, being
Forms of *do:* do, does, did	Others: could, should, would, may, might, must, can shall, will

Identifying Verbs

Underline the verb in each sentence. On the line to the right, label the verb **A** for action or **L** for linking.

1. My family likes the zoo in our city. _____

2. The kangaroos hop across the fields. _____

3. Baby kangaroos are safe inside their mothers' pouches. _____

4. I admire the big cats for their grace and power. _____

5. The monkeys easily swing from one tree to another. _____

6. The restless monkeys often sound noisy. _____

7. The prairie dogs scurry in and out of their holes in the ground. _____

8. Their movements are rapid. _____

Copyright © McDougal Littell/Houghton Mifflin Company.

CHAPTER 4

Lesson 1

What Is a Verb?

More Practice

A. Identifying Verbs

Underline the verb or verb phrase in each sentence. On the line to the right, label the verb with **A** for action or **L** for linking.

1. The koala bears have climbed the eucalyptus tree. _____

2. The peacock seemed more beautiful than before. _____

3. In the rain forest display at the zoo, the birds looked strange and exotic. _____

4. The goats in the children's zoo are hoping for treats. _____

5. Panda bears are rare. _____

6. Soon the hippopotamus will emerge from the murky water. _____

7. The hippopotamus can hold its breath for a long time. _____

8. The snake's skin feels rather smooth. _____

B. Identifying Helping Verbs and Main Verbs

In Exercise A, find the four sentences that use helping verbs. In the chart below, write those sentence numbers and the parts of each verb phrase in the correct columns.

Number	Helping Verb(s)	Main Verb
_____	_____	_____
_____	_____	_____
_____	_____	_____
_____	_____	_____

C. Using Verbs

In each sentence, replace the underlined verb with another verb that makes sense. Then write the sentence with the replacement verb.

1. Squirrels <u>go</u> up trees for protection. _____

_____

2. Ostriches <u>travel</u> at high speed for an animal. _____

_____

3. In caves, bats <u>rest</u> upside down. _____

_____

4. Spiders <u>remain</u> aware of all activity on their webs. _____

_____

Copyright © McDougal Littell/Houghton Mifflin Company.

CHAPTER 4

Lesson 1 **What Is a Verb?**   *Application*

A. Identifying and Replacing Verbs

In each sentence, underline the verb or verb phrase. If the verb is an action verb, rewrite the sentence with another action verb. If the original verb is a linking verb, simply write **Linking.**

1. Owls can turn their heads almost all the way around.

_____

2. A sea lion moves in the water with its flippers.

_____

3. Penguins look clumsy on land but graceful in the water.

_____

4. The shark chases the injured fish.

_____

5. Dolphin squeals sound high-pitched to human ears.

_____

6. Wildebeests travel each year from Kenya to northern South Africa.

_____

B. Using Verbs

On each line, write the action verb from the list that makes sense in the sentence and paragraph. Underline every linking verb.

to grow	to eat	to stay
to make	to bounce	to live

The killer whale is the largest member of the dolphin family. It

_____ in all of the oceans, especially in the colder waters. The

males can _____ as long as 32 feet; the females are usually

shorter, about 28 feet. While swimming, they _____ clicking

noises. The noises _____ off nearby objects, including other

animals, and the whales can interpret the echoes to know what is around

them. A killer whale _____ with the same group, or pod, of whales

for its entire life. The pods are often cooperative. Sometimes they hunt

together. Killer whales _____ fish, squid, birds, seals, and even

other whales.

Copyright © McDougal Littell/Houghton Mifflin Company.

CHAPTER 4

Lesson 2

Action Verbs and Objects

Teaching

Action verbs often require words that complete their meaning. These words are called **complements**. These complements are direct objects and indirect objects.

A **direct object** is a noun or pronoun that names the receiver of a verb's action. It answers the question *what* or *whom*.

> <u>Josephine</u> <u>writes</u> **novels**. (*What* does Josephine write? *Novels*.)

An **indirect object** tells *to what* or *whom* or *for what* or *whom* an action is done. Verbs that take indirect objects include *bring, give, lend, hand, make, send, show, teach, tell,* and *write.*

> <u>Tom</u> <u>gives</u> **friends** advice. (*To whom* does Tom give advice? *Friends*.)

Remember, if the preposition *to* or *for* appears before a word, the word is not an indirect object, but an object of a preposition.

Transitive and Intransitive Verbs An action verb that has a direct object is a **transitive verb.** An action verb that does not have a direct object is an **intransitive verb.**

Do not be confused when an intransitive verb is followed by an adverb. A direct object tells *what* or *whom;* an adverb tells *how, when, where,* or *to what extent.*

> <u>Jane</u> <u>writes</u> **stories**. (*What* does Jane write? *Stories*. Here *writes* is transitive.)

> <u>Jane</u> <u>writes</u> **well**. (*How* does Jane write? *Well*. Here *writes* is intransitive.)

Identifying Direct and Indirect Objects and Transitive and Intransitive Verbs

In each sentence, underline the verb or verb phrase. Above each boldfaced word write **DO, IO,** or **ADV** for direct object, indirect object, or adverb. On the line to the right, write whether the verb is **Transitive** or **Intransitive.**

1. Jonathan swims **well**. _____

2. He won the second-place **medal** in the interscholastic meet. _____

3. His friend Deborah baked **him** a chocolate **cake**. _____

4. Jonathan showed **her** the **medal**. _____

5. Thomas studied his **lessons** today. _____

6. He lost his **book**. _____

7. Mrs. Martin loaned **him** an extra **textbook**. _____

8. Helen sings **beautifully**. _____

9. She won the "New Voices" **competition**. _____

10. Her father bought **her** a **guitar**. _____

Copyright © McDougal Littell/Houghton Mifflin Company.

CHAPTER 4

Action Verbs and Objects

Lesson 2

More Practice

A. Identifying Direct and Indirect Objects and Transitive and Intransitive Verbs

In each sentence, underline the verb or verb phrase. Above each boldfaced word write **DO, IO,** or **ADV** for direct object, indirect object, or adverb. On the line at the right, write whether the verb is **Transitive** or **Intransitive.**

1. John received a silver **trophy.**   _____

2. The judges gave **him** a **check** for $100.   _____

3. The contestants all played **well.**   _____

4. Thomas won a silver **plate** in a different competition.   _____

5. Kim gave **Mariel** some good **advice** about the contest. _____

6. She told **Mariel** the judges' **preferences.**   _____

7. The operator gave the **students** complete **instructions.** _____

8. Nikki arrived **late** for the movie.   _____

9. Give the **ticket** to the usher.   _____

10. **What** did you have for dinner?   _____

B. Completing Transitive Verbs by Adding Direct Objects

Add a direct object to each of these sentences. You may also need to add adjectives or articles—*a, an,* or *the*—to the sentence.

1. The committee added _____ to the winning prize.

2. Thomas accepted _____.

3. Jonathan gave his brother _____.

4. Helen spent _____ for that table.

5. Maria wanted _____ for it.

6. The judges gave the acting troupe _____ for their performance.

7. Kyle told his mother _____ he had heard in class.

8. The thief took _____ from the cupboard.

9. The police noticed _____ outside the window.

10. Detectives questioned _____.

Copyright © McDougal Littell/Houghton Mifflin Company.

CHAPTER 4

Lesson 2 # Action Verbs and Objects   *Application*

A. Changing Intransitive Verbs to Transitive Verbs by Adding Direct Objects

The verb in each sentence below is an intransitive verb, without a direct object. Rewrite the sentence, using the same subject and verb but changing the rest of the sentence to make the verb transitive. Underline both the verb and the direct object that you add.

> **EXAMPLE** Mrs. Johnson dresses stylishly.
> *Mrs. Johnson dresses her twins in similar matching outfits.*

1. Anita ran well.

_____

2. Thomas played for a long time.

_____

3. Ms. Johnson sings with energy.

_____

4. This author writes for a large audience.

_____

B. Using Direct and Indirect Objects and Transitive and Intransitive Verbs

Write a paragraph about judging a contest and awarding prizes. In the paragraph, use at least four terms from each box. Use the verbs as either transitive or intransitive. Use the nouns and pronouns as direct objects or indirect objects. Underline every transitive verb in your paragraph.

Verbs				Nouns and Pronouns			
gave	guessed	called	thought	answer	question	friends	prize
read	told	showed	handed	audience	him	them	contestant
asked	tried	wrote	bet	it	rules	her	judges

_____

_____

_____

_____

_____

_____

CHAPTER 4

Copyright © McDougal Littell/Houghton Mifflin Company.

Lesson 3 # Linking Verbs and Predicate Words   *Teaching*

A **linking verb** connects the subject of a sentence to a word or words in the predicate. This word is called a **subject complement.** The subject complement identifies or describes the subject. Some common linking verbs are *is, feel, seem,* and *look.*

> Peanut butter <u>is</u> a popular American **food.**
> (The linking verb is *is;* the subject complement is *food.*)

> Peanut butter <u>looks</u> **gooey** in the jar.
> (The linking verb is *looks;* the subject complement is *gooey.*)

There are two kinds of subject complements.

A **predicate noun** is a noun or pronoun that follows a linking verb and identifies, renames, or defines the subject.

> Peanut butter is a tasty **snack.**
> (The predicate noun *snack* identifies the subject *peanut butter.*)

A **predicate adjective** is an adjective that follows a linking verb and describes or modifies the subject.

> Peanut butter on your hands feels **sticky.**
> (The predicate adjective *sticky* describes the subject *peanut butter.*)

Identifying Linking Verbs and Predicate Words

In each sentence, underline the subject once and the verb twice. Write the predicate word on the line to the right.

1. Peanut butter is rich in protein. _____

2. Ninety percent of its ingredients are crushed peanuts. _____

3. Another major ingredient is vegetable oil. _____

4. Peanuts are vegetables similar to beans. _____

5. They are not nuts. _____

6. Georgia is an important state for peanut production. _____

7. Peanuts look white at first. _____

8. They feel wet. _____

9. Peanuts are raw before roasting or boiling. _____

10. Raw peanuts taste bad. _____

11. The best quality peanuts become peanut butter. _____

12. Lower quality peanuts are an ingredient in shaving cream, paint, and shoe polish. _____

Copyright © McDougal Littell/Houghton Mifflin Company.

CHAPTER 4

Lesson 3 Linking Verbs and Predicate Words   *More Practice*

A. Identifying Linking Verbs and Predicate Words

In each sentence, underline the subject once and the verb twice. Write the predicate word on the line to the right.

1. Milk is a dairy product. _____

2. Lactose is a sugar in milk. _____

3. Many adults around the world are allergic to lactose and milk. _____

4. Cold milk tastes great on a hot day. _____

5. A creamery is a butter and cheese factory. _____

6. Pasteurization is an essential process in milk production. _____

7. Yogurt is milk with added bacteria. _____

8. Yogurt sometimes tastes tart. _____

9. Yogurt with fruit often tastes sweet. _____

10. Churned cream becomes butter. _____

B. Using Predicate Words

Complete each sentence by writing a predicate complement on the line. In the parentheses following the sentence, write **PN** if you added a predicate noun and **PA** if you added a predicate adjective.

1. Oranges, tangerines, and lemons are _____. (___)

2. The red tomatoes in that bin appear _____. (___)

3. That salad of lettuce, cucumbers, and carrots looks _____. (___)

4. The food pyramid is a _____ that illustrates the types of foods and the number of servings people should eat daily. (___)

5. The vegetable beef soup simmering on the stove smells _____. (___)

6. Popcorn with just a little bit of butter is a healthy _____. (___)

7. People who do not eat meat are _____. (___)

8. Sweet potatoes taste _____ with turkey, cranberries, and stuffing. (___)

9. People sharing a meal together usually feel _____. (___)

Copyright © McDougal Littell/Houghton Mifflin Company.

CHAPTER 4

Linking Verbs and Predicate Words *Application*

A. Identifying and Using Linking Verbs and Predicate Words

In each sentence, underline the subject once and the verb twice. Write the predicate word on the line to the right. After the predicate word, identify it by writing **PN** for predicate noun or **PA** for predicate adjective.

EXAMPLE <u>Carrots</u> <u>are</u> vegetables. *vegetables, PN*

1. Canned foods are safe for all. _____

2. Corned beef is delicious with scrambled eggs. _____

3. Dried foods are good meals for campers. _____

4. For many campers, a can opener is an essential tool. _____

5. Banana chips are dried food. _____

6. Powdered drinks are handy for backpackers. _____

7. Fresh food becomes unsafe after a few days without refrigeration. _____

8. Bottled water is popular with athletes and travelers. _____

B. Identifying and Using Linking Verbs and Predicate Words

Rewrite each predicate word in Exercise A. When possible, replace predicate nouns with predicate adjectives, and predicate adjectives with predicate nouns. Change other words in the predicate as needed.

EXAMPLE Carrots are *part of my beef stew.* OR
Carrots are *delicious.*

1. Canned foods are _____.

2. Corned beef is _____.

3. Dried foods are _____.

4. For many campers, a can opener is _____.

5. Banana chips are _____.

6. Powdered drinks are _____.

7. Fresh food becomes _____.

8. Bottled water is _____.

Copyright © McDougal Littell/Houghton Mifflin Company.

Lesson 4 Principal Parts of Verbs

Teaching

Every verb has four basic forms called its principal parts: the **present,** the **present participle,** the **past,** and the **past participle.** With helping verbs, these four parts make all the tenses and forms of the verb.

I **watch** football. (present)
I am **watching** the game today. (present participle)
I **watched** the game last night. (past)
I have **watched** three games this weekend. (past participle)

The Four Principal Parts of a Verb			
Present	**Present Participle**	**Past**	**Past Participle**
watch	(is) watching	watched	(has) watched
wait	(is) waiting	waited	(has) waited

There are two kinds of verbs: regular and irregular.

A **regular verb** is a verb whose past and past participle are formed by adding *-ed* or *-d* to the present. The present participle is formed by adding *-ing* to the present. Spelling changes are needed in some words, for example, *carry–carried.*

Present	**Present Participle**	**Past**	**Past Participle**
wait	(is) wait + **ing**	wait + **ed**	(has) wait + **ed**

Irregular verbs are discussed in the next lesson.

Identifying Forms of Regular Verbs

In each sentence, identify the underlined principal part of the verb. Write **Pres., Pres. Part., Past,** or **Past Part.** on the line to the right to identify the present, present participle, past, or past participle form.

EXAMPLE Susan has <u>decided</u> not to go along. *Past Part.*

1. Vivaldi <u>lived</u> in Venice in the early 18th century. _____

2. His music <u>features</u> strong rhythm and melody. _____

3. Interest in his music is <u>growing</u> at this time. _____

4. The orchestra is <u>playing</u> one of his pieces this evening. _____

5. Vivaldi <u>composed</u> about 450 concertos. _____

6. One critic has <u>suggested</u> Vivaldi composed just one concerto 450 times. _____

7. However, most critics <u>consider</u> that opinion unjust. _____

8. Have you <u>listened</u> to *The Four Seasons* all the way through? _____

Copyright © McDougal Littell/Houghton Mifflin Company.

CHAPTER 4

Lesson 4 Principal Parts of Verbs   *More Practice*

A. Identifying Forms of Regular Verbs

In each sentence, identify the underlined principal part of the verb. Write **Pres.,**
Pres. Part., Past, or **Past Part.** on the line to the right to identify the present,
present participle, past, or past participle form.

1. The orchestra is <u>performing</u> *Peter and the Wolf* at the children's
concert today.   _____

2. Mr. Ortiz is <u>taking</u> his class to the children's concert this afternoon.   _____

3. Mr. Ortiz <u>plays</u> the violin in a local orchestra.   _____

4. He has <u>appeared</u> with his orchestra in holiday concerts at the band shell. _____

5. The young audience <u>enjoyed</u> the concert.   _____

6. After the concert, Mr. Ortiz <u>asked</u> the class to name their favorite piece. _____

7. He has <u>asked</u> the same question of other classes.   _____

8. Every year, the children <u>answer</u> the same way.   _____

9. Mr. Ortiz <u>guesses</u> that some pieces appeal to young people more
than others.   _____

10. Most young listeners <u>like</u> lively music with strong melodies.   _____

B. Writing the Correct Forms of Verbs

Decide which form of the verb given in parentheses is needed. Write the correct
form on the line.

    EXAMPLE Ashley is (get) onto the bus. *getting*

1. The librarian is (look) for the book on the shelves.   _____

2. The store clerk (promise) that your gift would be here by your birthday. _____

3. Ms. Kohl has (raise) vegetables in her backyard garden for 20 years. _____

4. Christopher is (expect) a call from his cousin.   _____

5. At the football game last night, Gina (shout) and cheered.   _____

6. The package you sent for earlier has finally (arrive).   _____

7. To get to my house, (follow) these directions.   _____

8. Audiences always (laugh) at silly jokes.   _____

9. Some astronomers are (listen) to sounds from outer space.   _____

Copyright © McDougal Littell/Houghton Mifflin Company.

CHAPTER 4

Name _____ Date _____

Principal Parts of Verbs   *Application*

A. Writing the Correct Forms of Verbs

Decide which form of the verb given in parentheses is needed. Write the correct form
on the line. Then identify which form you have used. Write **Pres., Pres. Part., Past,** or
Past Part. to identify the present, present participle, past, or past participle form.

> **EXAMPLE** Someone has (remove) the spare tire. *removed, Past Part.*

1. No one is (doubt) your good intentions. _____

2. Matt (support) the winning candidate in the last election. _____

3. We all had (hope) for good weather for yesterday's picnic. _____

4. Vivaldi (compose) his sonatas for his students to perform. _____

5. The interviewer is (ask) the movie star about her upcoming film. _____

6. The scientist has (study) tropical insects for years. _____

7. Laura is (plan) on finishing the project today. _____

8. The family (hurry) through breakfast every morning. _____

9. The announcer has (call) that person's name at least three times. _____

10. A few moments ago, the rain finally (stop). _____

B. Supplying Verbs in the Correct Forms

Almost all the main verbs are missing from this paragraph. On each blank line,
choose the verb that makes sense in the story. Be sure to use the correct form of
the verb.

to listen	to live	to work	to play	to join
to learn	to compose	to instruct	to fill	

     Johann Sebastian Bach was a musical genius and a devoted family

man. Bach _____ in Germany from 1685 to 1750. You may have

_____ to some of his music if you have ever gone to an orchestra

concert. He _____ hundreds of pieces over his long life. Bach

must have _____ how to play the harpsichord when he was very

young. When he was only 18, he _____ an orchestra as a violinist

and soon started writing his own music. Bach had a large family: 7 children

with his first wife and 13 children with his second wife. He _____

hard to support them. He _____ the organ in churches and

_____ students. His music is _____ with energy and

enthusiasm.

Copyright © McDougal Littell/Houghton Mifflin Company.

Lesson 5 ## Irregular Verbs   *Teaching*

Irregular verbs are verbs whose past and past participle are not formed by adding *-ed* or *-d* to the present. The five sections of this chart show different patterns used to form the past and past participles of many irregular verbs.

	Present	Past	Past Participle
Group 1 Forms of the present, past, and past participle are all same	hit hurt let put set split	hit hurt let put set split	(have) hit (have) hurt (have) let (have) put (have) set (have) split
Group 2 The forms of past and past participle are same	bring catch lead sit	brought caught led sat	(have) brought (have) caught (have) led (have) sat
Group 3 The past participle is formed by adding *-n* or *-en* to the past.	break lie speak steal wear	broke lay spoke stole wore	(have) broken (have) lain (have) spoken (have) stolen (have) worn

	Present	Past	Past Participle
Group 4 The past participle is formed from the present, often by adding *-n, -ne,* or *-en.*	do drive eat fall go know see take	did drove ate fell went knew saw took	(have) done (have) driven (have) eaten (have) fallen (have) gone (have) known (have) seen (have) taken
Group 5 The last vowel changes from *i* in the present to *a* in the past and to *u* in the past participle.	begin drink ring swim	began drank rang swam	(have) begun (have) drunk (have) rung (have) sum

The different forms of the verb *be* do not follow any pattern.

Present	Past	Past Participle
am, is, are	was, were	(have) been

Using the Correct Forms of Irregular Verbs

Underline the correct verb form in parentheses to complete each sentence.

1. With wings on his hat and feet, Mercury (ran, run) incredibly fast.

2. In the early 1900s, people (saw, seen) silent movies at little theaters called nickelodeons.

3. How many different languages are (spoke, spoken) in Europe?

4. Have you ever (took, taken) care of a pet?

5. The baseball game (begin, began) an hour late because of the rain.

6. Have officials (chose, chosen) the city for the next Olympics?

7. Daryl (bring, brought) the stray cat to the animal shelter.

8. The Greek gods and goddesses (drank, drunk) nectar.

9. The magician (did, done) a card trick and a disappearing act.

10. The bear (come, came) out of its den in the spring.

Copyright © McDougal Littell/Houghton Mifflin Company.

Lesson 5 Irregular Verbs

More Practice

A. Using the Correct Forms of Irregular Verbs

Underline the correct verb form in parentheses to complete each sentence.

1. Benjamin Franklin had (flew, flown) a kite during a thunderstorm.

2. During the parade, confetti (fell, fallen) on the floats.

3. U.S. astronauts (went, gone) to the moon six times between 1969 and 1972.

4. Pecos Bill (rode, ridden) a cyclone across three states.

5. Rachel Carson (wrote, written) about the sea and the environment.

6. After the wedding, the guests (threw, thrown) rice at the bride and groom.

7. We have (brang, brought) our finest vegetables to the garden exhibit.

8. The spider has (catched, caught) a fly in its web.

9. Mark has (swim, swum) across the lake twice this week.

10. Robin Hood (stole, stolen) from the rich and gave to the poor.

B. Writing the Correct Forms of Verbs

Decide which form is needed: the present participle, the past, or the past participle of each verb given in parentheses. Write the correct form on the line.

   EXAMPLE The thieves have (steal) our sandwiches. *stolen*

1. Nora (see) the toy exhibit at the museum. _____

2. People (speak) French in parts of Canada. _____

3. That character has (say) "Good grief" several times. _____

4. The tiny pin (burst) the large balloon. _____

5. In the science fiction story, computers had (take) over the world. _____

6. My brother (teach) me to change a flat bicycle tire. _____

7. The valuable painting had (lie) in an old barn for years. _____

8. I have (give) you all the hints I can. _____

9. My friend has (write) a new short story. _____

10. I have (make) my final decision. _____

Copyright © McDougal Littell/Houghton Mifflin Company.

Lesson 5 Irregular Verbs

Application

A. Writing the Correct Forms of Verbs

Decide which form of the verb given in parentheses is needed. Write the correct form on the line. Then identify which form you used by writing **Past** or **PP** for *past participle.*

EXAMPLE The choir has (sing) the school song. *sung, PP*

1. The wild horse has (throw) the cowboy off its back. _____

2. The choir has (sing) the final song of the program. _____

3. Charles Lindbergh (fly) nonstop across the Atlantic Ocean in 1927. _____

4. During space missions, some astronauts have (fall) asleep while floating in the air. _____

5. Snow White (eat) the poison apple. _____

6. She (fall) into a deep sleep. _____

7. I had (tear) my jacket on a nail. _____

8. It looks like my jeans (shrink) while they were in the dryer. _____

9. The explorers (ride) on camels as they crossed the desert. _____

10. The sheriff and his deputies (go) after the bandits. _____

B. Proofreading for the Correct Forms of Verbs

Draw a line through each incorrect verb form in this paragraph. Draw this proofreading symbol ⌃ next to the error and, in the spaces between lines of type, write the correct form of the verb.

EXAMPLE Have you ever ~~saw~~ ⌃a dinosaur skeleton?
                              seen

Last week our class goed to the science museum on a field trip. We seen

a dinosaur exhibit with lifelike models of dinosaurs that the museum guide

letted us touch. The skin feeled really rough and strange. Ms. Anderson asked

who knowed the name of the dinosaur with the three horns, so I said,

"*Triceratops.*" I was right. I have knowed about *Triceratops* for years. Our field

trip great. As soon as I come back to the school, I begun reading a good book

about dinosaurs. If I hadn't went to the museum, I might never have thinked

about dinosaurs, but now I am fascinated by them.

Copyright © McDougal Littell/Houghton Mifflin Company.

CHAPTER 4

Lesson 6

Simple Tenses

Teaching

A **tense** is a verb form that shows the time of an action or condition. Verbs have three **simple tenses:** the present, the past, and the future.

The **present tense** shows an action or condition that occurs now. The **past tense** shows an action or condition that was completed in the past. The **future tense** shows an action or condition that will occur in the future.

Present	Lydia **dusts** cabinets. She **is** helpful.
Past	Lydia **dusted** cabinets. She **was** helpful.
Future	Lydia **will dust** cabinets. She **will be** helpful.

The progressive form of a verb shows an action or condition that is in progress.

Present Progressive	Lydia **is dusting** cabinets. She **is being** helpful.
Past Progressive	Lydia **was dusting** cabinets. She **was being** helpful.
Future Progressive	Lydia **will be dusting** cabinets. She **will be being** helpful.

The **present tense** is the present principal part of the verb. The **past tense** is the past principal part. To form the **future tense,** add *will* to the present principal part.

Tense	Singular	Plural
Present	I dust / you dust / he, she, it dusts	we dust / you dust / they dust
Past	I dusted / you dusted / he, she, it dusted	we dusted / you dusted / they dusted
Future	I will dust / you will dust / he, she, it will dust	we will dust / you will dust / they will dust

Form the **present, past,** and **future progressives** by adding the present, past, and future forms of the verb *be* to the present participle, as in *I am dusting, I was dusting,* and *I will be dusting.*

Recognizing the Simple Tenses

Identify the tense of each underlined verb. On the line to the right, label the tense: **Pres., Past, F., Pres. P., Past P.,** or **F. P.** for present, past, future, present progressive, past progressive, or future progressive.

1. The woman next door <u>is painting</u> her house. _____

2. Henri <u>paints</u> pictures. _____

3. Jon <u>washed</u> the car before you got here. _____

4. He <u>was waxing</u> it when you arrived. _____

5. We <u>will clean</u> the carpets. _____

6. <u>Will</u> you still <u>be working</u> when my guests arrive? _____

7. We <u>will work</u> until you tell us to stop. _____

8. First, I <u>want</u> you to wash some windows. _____

Copyright © McDougal Littell/Houghton Mifflin Company.

CHAPTER 4

Lesson 6 — Simple Tenses

Lesson 6

More Practice

A. Recognizing the Simple Tenses

Identify the tense of each underlined verb. On the line, label the tense: **Present, Past, Future,** or **Present P., Past P.,** or **Future P.** for present, past, or future progressive.

1. We <u>clean</u> the house from top to bottom every spring and fall. _____

2. *Is* Nelson <u>washing</u> the windows? _____

3. When I saw him last, he <u>was dozing</u> in the hammock. _____

4. He <u>works</u> hard. _____

5. Mary <u>vacuumed</u> the downstairs. _____

6. I <u>will sweep</u> the kitchen floor next. _____

7. I <u>needed</u> some help with the dishes. _____

8. I <u>will wash</u>, and you can dry. _____

9. We <u>will be cleaning</u> for another two hours. _____

10. <u>Will</u> Nelson <u>be helping</u> us? _____

B. Using the Simple Tenses

In each item, provide the requested form of the verb in parentheses.

1. (*start,* future progressive) The workers _____ the job tomorrow.

2. (*finish,* future) They _____ it within a week.

3. (*paint,* past) They _____ Ms. Antonelli's porch in two days.

4. (*scrape,* present) Before they paint, they _____ the old paint.

5. (*scrape,* past progressive) They _____ Ms. Antonelli's porch earlier.

6. (*hire,* past) We _____ professionals .

7. (*offer,* future) I _____ them lunch in a few hours.

Copyright © McDougal Littell/Houghton Mifflin Company.

CHAPTER 4

CHAPTER 4

Lesson 6

Simple Tenses

Application

A. Correcting Simple Tenses of Verbs

Although the times referred to in this paragraph vary from the past to the future, all of its verbs are in the present tense. Rewrite the paragraph, correcting verb tenses as needed. Use progressive tenses if the action is, was, or will be in progress. Underline every verb.

Next summer we paint the house. We use at least 20 gallons of blue and five gallons of white paint. We should make sure the brushes and buckets that we use to paint the garage last year are available. Maybe we need a few more brushes. At the end of last summer, we borrow each other's brushes. Also, next summer, we need more scrapers. Last summer, we lend two to Mr. Vincent, and he never return them.

_____

_____

_____

_____

_____

_____

_____

_____

B. Using Verb Forms Correctly

For each verb on the list, write the form that is requested in parentheses. Then write a paragraph about a topic of your choice that uses at least four of the phrases. Make sure all verb forms are used correctly.

(play, present) I _____   (plan, present progressive) I _____

(run, past) I _____   (train, future progressive) I _____

(compete, future) I _____   (work, past progressive) I _____

_____

_____

_____

_____

_____

Copyright © McDougal Littell/Houghton Mifflin Company.

Copyright © McDougal Littell/Houghton Mifflin Company.

Lesson 7 — Perfect Tenses

Teaching

The **present perfect tense** shows an action or condition that began in the past and continues into the present.

    Present Perfect Carl **has practiced** piano <u>every day this week.</u>

The **past perfect tense** shows an action or condition in the past that came before another action or condition in the past.

    Past Perfect   Carl **had practiced** <u>before Maria arrived</u>.

The **future perfect tense** shows an action or condition in the future that will occur before another action or condition in the future.

    Future Perfect   Carl **will have practiced** <u>tomorrow</u> before Maria arrives.

To form the **present perfect, past perfect,** and **future perfect tenses,** add *has, have, had,* or *will have* to the past participle of the verb.

Tense	Singular	Plural
Present Perfect *has* or *have* + past participle	I have practiced you have practiced he, she, it has practiced	we have practiced you had practiced they have practiced
Past Perfect *had* + past participle	I had practiced you had practiced he, she, it had practiced	we had practiced you had practiced they had practiced
Future Perfect *will* + *have* + past participle	I will have practiced you will have practiced he, she, it will have practiced	we will have practiced you will have practiced they will have practiced

Recognizing the Perfect Tenses

Underline the verb in each sentence. On the line, write the tense of the verb: present perfect, past perfect, or future perfect.

1. I have ruined my good suit. _____

2. Haley will have left before Joshua's arrival. _____

3. Christy has begun the last chapter of the book. _____

4. We had started the fire well before dark. _____

5. By noon, I will have chopped wood for the fire. _____

6. By nightfall, six inches of snow had fallen. _____

7. We have checked all the calculations. _____

8. The reporter had submitted her article before the six o'clock news broadcast. _____

9. Before the accident, Megan had entered the competition. _____

10. I will have learned my part before the first rehearsal. _____

CHAPTER 4

Lesson 7 # Perfect Tenses   *More Practice*

A. Recognizing the Perfect Tenses

Underline the verb in each sentence. On the line, write the tense of the verb: present perfect, past perfect, or future perfect.

1. Emma had seemed blue before the happy news.   _____

2. Julie has biked to school every day this month.   _____

3. Julie will have ridden 500 miles by the end of the year.   _____

4. Bill has read that book three times.   _____

5. Have you ridden the fastest roller coaster at the amusement park? _____

6. Many pioneers had written about their experiences in diaries. _____

7. At this rate, we will have finished the book by the end of the term. _____

8. We have tried every possible solution.   _____

9. The spy has stolen secret formulas from the scientist's lab. _____

10. The time travelers had visited the era of the dinosaurs.   _____

B. Forming the Perfect Tenses

Complete each sentence by writing the form of the verb indicated in parentheses.

1. (*finish,* past perfect) The family _____ the board game before dinner.

2. (*move,* future perfect) Our neighbors _____ before next summer.

3. (*score,* future perfect) At this rate, the team _____ 40 points by halftime.

4. (*study,* present perfect) We _____ for more than two hours.

5. (*ask,* past perfect) The interviewer _____ that question twice already.

6. (*do,* future perfect) I _____ most of the research by this weekend.

7. (*go,* present perfect) Ed_____ to bed early every night since he got a cold.

8. (*walk,* future perfect) By the end of the program, they _____ 100 miles.

9. (*speak,* past perfect) Susan B. Anthony _____ about women's rights for years.

10. (*save,* present perfect) Mom _____ a piece of apple pie for you.

Copyright © McDougal Littell/Houghton Mifflin Company.

Lesson 7 Perfect Tenses

Application

A. Using Verb Tenses

A student on a school field trip to Washington, D.C., wrote the following letter to her parents. Supply verbs to the letter in the tenses indicated in parentheses. Choose verbs from the list below.

explore   travel   visit   want   walk

The trip has been wonderful so far. We (present perfect)

_____ so many places! I (past perfect)

_____ to see them for a long time. We (present perfect)

_____ everywhere—along the mall and from the mall to

the Lincoln and Jefferson memorials. By Friday we (future perfect)

_____ the Smithsonian Institution and the National Gallery

of Art too. Before we come home, we (future perfect)

_____ by bus to the Gettysburg Battlefield, which is only

a short distance from Washington, Ms. Johnson says.

B. Using Verb Tenses

Think of a trip you have made or would like to make. Write sentences about that trip, using the following verbs in the tenses indicated in parentheses.

1. visit (future) _____

_____

2. travel (present perfect) _____

_____

3. hike (future perfect) _____

_____

4. look (past perfect) _____

_____

5. eat (future perfect) _____

_____

6. learn (past perfect) _____

_____

Copyright © McDougal Littell/Houghton Mifflin Company.

CHAPTER 4

Lesson 8 # Using Verb Tenses   *Teaching*

In writing and speaking, you use the tenses of verbs to indicate when events happen. Changing tenses indicates a change in time. If you do not need to indicate a change in time between two actions, keep the tenses of the two verbs the same.

The Present Tenses These tenses show events occurring in the present time:

Present	Action occurs in the present.	watch, watches
Present perfect	Action placed in a period of time leading up to the present.	has watched, have watched
Present progressive	Action is in progress now.	is watching, are watching

The Past Tenses These tenses show events occurring in a past time:

Past	Action began and ended in the past.	watched
Past perfect	Action began and ended before another event in the past.	had watched
Past progressive	Action in the past was ongoing.	was watching

The Future Tenses These tenses show events occurring in a future time:

Future	Action will occur in the future.	will watch
Future perfect	Action will occur in the future, before another action in the future.	will have watched
Future progressive	Action in the future will be ongoing.	will be watching

Using Verb Tenses

Underline the verb form in parentheses that correctly completes each sentence.

1. When Charles Lindbergh was born, no one (had heard, will hear) of jets, or even of motorized airplanes.

2. Young Charles was born in 1902 and (was growing, grew) up on a farm.

3. Even as a child, Charles (showed, is showing) a love for engines.

4. Later, although he (has studied, had studied) engineering in college, he was more interested in flying planes.

5. Charles (will have become, became) a good pilot.

6. In 1919 he (learned, is learning) about a contest in which he could win $25,000.

7. All he (had, has) to do was fly a plane nonstop from New York to Paris.

8. No one (is doing, had done) that before.

9. Charles Lindbergh (was flying, flew) the 3,600 miles in 33 1/2 hours.

10. People in Paris (had been waiting, will have been waiting) for him for hours, and they met his plane with a huge celebration.

Copyright © McDougal Littell/Houghton Mifflin Company.

CHAPTER 4

Lesson 8 · Using Verb Tenses   *More Practice*

A. Using Verb Tenses

Underline the verb form in parentheses that correctly completes each sentence.

1. People who love mysteries (were talking, have been talking) about Amelia Earhart for several decades.

2. What about Ms. Earhart (makes, will be making) her so fascinating?

3. Amelia Earhart (was, has been) one of the first well-known woman pilots.

4. She (has worked, had worked) as a nurse and as a social worker before learning to fly a plane.

5. In 1932, Amelia flew solo across the Atlantic Ocean just as Charles Lindbergh (was doing, had done) a few years earlier.

6. Before her solo trip across the Atlantic, Amelia (will be, had been) the first female passenger on a flight from Newfoundland to Europe.

7. Amelia (was becoming, is becoming) more and more interested in a flight around the world.

8. In 1937, she and an experienced copilot (have begun, began) their flight around the globe.

9. They were near the Howland Islands in the Pacific Ocean when they (have vanished, vanished) into thin air.

10. Whatever (will be happening, happened) to Amelia Earhart?

B. Correcting Sentence Order

The sentences of this story are out of order. Read the story. Use the verb tenses and context to determine the correct order. Then rewrite the story in paragraph form below or on a separate sheet of paper, with the sentences in correct order.

> On a camping trip last summer, my father and I were cooking a chowder over the campfire.
> We must have watched the sunset a little too long.
> While the pot was cooling, we took a hike down to the lake to watch the sunset.
> If we take a walk before dinner on our next camping trip, we will definitely bring Gemini along with us.
> Dad took the pot of boiling chowder off the fire to cool.
> When we got back, Gemini, our dog, was lapping up the last of the chowder.

_____

_____

_____

_____

_____

Copyright © McDougal Littell/Houghton Mifflin Company.

CHAPTER 4

Lesson 8 Using Verb Tenses   *Application*

A. Correcting Verb Tenses

Each underlined verb is in an incorrect tense. Write the correct form of the verb on the line.

1. The students **have entered** the building only a few moments before the fire alarm sounded.   _____

2. If you want to win the prize, you **are answering** this simple question.   _____

3. After the snow finally stopped falling, children all over the city **will be playing** in it for the rest of the day.   _____

4. If that swimmer keeps us her pace, she **was breaking** the world record.   _____

5. Although the little girl **is hearing** the story before, she listened attentively.   _____

6. When a pedestrian **crossed** a street, he or she should look both ways.   _____

7. Because Gina **is forgetting** her lunch four times in a row, Mom handed it to her at the door.   _____

8. When the actor forgot his words, a prompter behind the curtain **has whispered** them to him.   _____

B. Correcting Verb Tenses

Some of the verbs in this paragraph are in the wrong tense. Decide which verbs must be changed. Then rewrite the paragraph on a separate sheet of paper, correcting those verbs. Underline the verbs you have changed.

> One of the great mysteries in American history will be the fate of the colonists of Roanoke Island. In 1585, John White was leaving the small colony of 115 people and headed back to England for supplies. A war has interfered with his return, however. When White will return five years later, no one lives in the colony anymore. On a tree has been carved the word *CROATOAN*. White and the other puzzled rescuers do not know what that word meant. All that was certain was that all the people were gone. Were they dead? Have they been captured by the Spanish? Had they joined a nearby tribe? Their disappearance had been a mystery ever since.

CHAPTER 4

Copyright © McDougal Littell/Houghton Mifflin Company.

Lesson 9

Troublesome Verb Pairs   *Teaching*

Do not confuse these pairs of verbs. Read how they differ, and study the chart.

lie/lay *Lie* means "to rest or recline." It does not take an object.
Lay means "to put or place something." It does take an object

set/sit *Sit* means "to be in a seat" or "to rest." It does not take an object.
Set means "to put or place something." It does take an object.

rise/raise *Rise* means "to move upward" or "to go up." It does not take an object.
Raise means "to lift (something) up." It usually takes an object.

learn/teach *Learn* means "to gain knowledge or skill."
Teach means "to help someone learn."

Verb	Present	Past	Past Participle
Lie	**lie** Rover lies at my feet.	**lay** Rover lay here earlier.	**lain** Rover has lain there.
Lay	**lay(s)** Ted lays a cup here.	**laid** He laid a cup there.	**laid** He has laid two cups.
Sit	**sit** The cat sits there.	**sat** The cat sat there.	**sat** The cat has sat there.
Set	**set** She sets the box down.	**set** She set it down before.	**set** She has set it down.
Rise	**rise** We rise at 8 A.M.	**rose** We rose early.	**risen** You have risen early.
Raise	**raise** Lee raises her hand.	**raised** Lee raised it.	**raised** Lee has raised it.
Learn	**learn** I learn to add.	**learn** I learned that before.	**learn** I have learned that.
Teach	**teach** He teaches math.	**taught** He taught math.	**taught** He has taught math.

Using Troublesome Verbs Correctly

Underline the correct verb in parentheses.

1. The islanders (learn, teach) their toddlers about fish.
2. The students (learned, taught) a valuable lesson from their wilderness experience.
3. The campers were (lying, laying) on the ground.
4. A Persian rug with beautiful patterns (lay, laid) on the floor.
5. Alice (sat, set) with three odd characters at a tea party.
6. (Set, Sit) the time machine to the year 2020.
7. The temperature has (raised, risen) four degrees in the past hour.
8. Someone (rose, raised) the bar.
9. The animal trainer (teaches, learns) the circus elephants tricks.
10. The tide is (rising, raising) along the shore.
11. After the ceremony, the queen (lay, laid) her crown in its glass case.
12. Did you (sat, set) your books on the piano bench yesterday?

Copyright © McDougal Littell/Houghton Mifflin Company.

CHAPTER 4

Lesson 9

Troublesome Verb Pairs

More Practice

A. Using Troublesome Verbs Correctly

Underline the correct verb in parentheses.

1. The island of Hawaii (rose, raised) from volcanoes under the sea.

2. The movie theaters (rose, raised) the price of tickets.

3. Anne Sullivan Macy (learned, taught) Helen Keller how to speak, read, and write.

4. Astronauts are (learned, taught) to survive in space.

5. The campers (sat, set) around the fire and listened to ghost stories.

6. The table in the museum was (sat, set) with silverware from the 1700s.

7. Last month, the construction workers (lay, laid) the foundation of the skyscraper.

8. My lazy old cat (lies, lays) in the sun.

9. Lin (rose, raised) important questions about the future of our planet.

10. Girls in colonial America (learned, taught) spinning and weaving from their mothers.

B. Correcting Troublesome Verbs

Examine the boldfaced verb in each of the following sentences. If the verb is not correct, write the proper verb on the line. If the verb is correct, write **Correct**.

1. King Arthur **learned** about the magic sword from Merlin the magician. _____

2. My older sister **learned** me to read when I was in kindergarten. _____

3. Marie **lay** down and took a nap on the sofa. _____

4. Where have you **lain** my magazine? _____

5. The science fiction story is **setting** on the coffee table. _____

6. Did you **sit** the keys down on the kitchen table? _____

7. The hot-air balloon **raises** above the treetops. _____

8. Scrooge **rose** Bob Cratchit's salary at the end of *A Christmas Carol*. _____

9. We **raised** the flag in front of our school this morning. _____

10. Please **sit** down over by the sofa. _____

Copyright © McDougal Littell/Houghton Mifflin Company.

CHAPTER 4

Troublesome Verb Pairs

Application

Lesson 9

A. Correcting Troublesome Verbs

Examine the boldfaced verb in each of the following sentences. If the verb is not correct, write the proper verb on the line. If the verb is correct, write **Correct.**

1. Please **set** the box down on the table. _____

2. Do not **sit** your books on the couch. _____

3. Will you **teach** me to play the flute? _____

4. David is **learning** me to fix bicycles. _____

5. Do not **rise** your hand until the speaker is finished. _____

6. Grandmother **set** in her chair to read us a story. _____

7. Max **raised** the hood of his car to signal that he needed help. _____

8. Yesterday, the architect **lay** out the blueprints for the house. _____

9. If you leave your papers **laying** around, the baby might get them. _____

10. Farmers in south-central Canada **raise** wheat. _____

B. Using Troublesome Verbs Correctly

The following sentences contain five incorrectly used verbs. Rewrite the paragraph below, correcting all five errors.

When I was just a little boy, my Uncle Fred learned me how to fish.
I remember the first morning. We raised at dawn and had a breakfast of
scrambled eggs, toast, and coffee (hot chocolate for me). Then we set in my
uncle's boat for two hours before we got a bite. But when the fish did start to
bite, things got exciting. In an hour, we had caught our limit. After a while,
I laid down in the bottom of the boat and slept for an hour. Maybe I will learn
my own son how to fish someday.

_____

_____

_____

_____

_____

_____

_____

Copyright © McDougal Littell/Houghton Mifflin Company.

CHAPTER 4

Lesson 1

What Is an Adjective?

Teaching

An **adjective** is a word that modifies, or describes, a noun or a pronoun.

Adjectives	
What kind?	**sunny** day, **cool** evening
Which one or ones?	**nearest** umbrella, **next** day
How many or how much?	**many** waves, **90** degrees

Articles

The most commonly used adjectives are the articles *a, an,* and *the*. *A* and *an* refer to someone or something in general. Use *a* before a word beginning with a consonant and *an* before a word beginning with a vowel.

<u>A</u> day at the beach can be <u>an</u> interesting experience.

The points out a specific person, place, thing, or idea.

Did you bring <u>the</u> suntan lotion?

Proper Adjectives

Many adjectives are formed from common nouns, such as *sandy* from *sand*. Proper adjectives are formed from proper nouns. **Proper adjectives** are always capitalized.

Proper Nouns	Proper Adjectives
Asia	Asian
Mexico	Mexican

Identifying Adjectives

Underline all the adjectives, including articles, in each sentence.

1. Many families headed for a favorite beach last week during the hot weather.
2. One particular family went to a pleasant beach on the ocean.
3. They brought along the Chinese umbrella they always take.
4. The umbrella protected them from the harmful rays of the sun.
5. The young children spent time playing in the fine sand.
6. The oldest boy, Alexander, jumped in and out of the large waves.
7. The cold water was a welcome relief from the steamy day.
8. After several hours the family decided it was time to get some food.
9. They walked over to the Boardwalk where they found an Italian restaurant.
10. They walked in and ordered a huge platter of 36 shrimp.
11. Afterwards, they walked along the rocky edge of the beach.
12. The parents admired the beautiful lighthouse in the distance.
13. An quick game of volleyball topped off the day.
14. On the way home, the weary family talked about their wonderful day.

Copyright © McDougal Littell/Houghton Mifflin Company.

CHAPTER 5

Name _____ Date _____

What Is an Adjective?

More Practice

A. Identifying Adjectives and the Words They Modify

Underline each adjective once and the word it modifies twice. Circle the proper adjectives. Ignore the articles.

1. Colorful Navajo blankets are sold on Indian reservations.
2. Most American colonists ate bread and cold meat for breakfast.
3. The powerful winds of a tornado blew off the roofs of many houses.
4. Sharp fangs and huge eyes were painted on the Chinese mask.
5. The Arabian desert contains the remains of ancient cities.
6. In Greek mythology the Minotaur was a horrible monster.
7. In old Western movies, good cowboys wear white hats, and bad cowboys wear black hats.
8. Hawaiian leis are necklaces of beautiful flowers such as orchids.
9. The Alaskan pipeline took many years to complete.
10. Egyptian slaves helped build the gigantic pyramids.

B. Writing Adjectives

Write an adjective to complete each sentence.

EXAMPLE The _____*tall*_____ chairs on the beach are for the lifeguards.

1. To escape from the _____ weather, I head to the beach.

2. The _____ beach to my house is about half an hour away.

3. I have to be careful when I am in the sun because I have _____ skin.

4. So, I always apply plenty of _____ lotion.

5. I like to look for _____ shells along the beach.

6. Often, my friends and I will organize a _____ game of volleyball.

7. Ever since the _____ competition I entered five years ago, I have competed in the annual sand castle competition.

8. Mom spends most of her time at the beach reading a _____ book.

9. I usually see _____ seagulls flying around the water's edge.

10. Near the end of the day, I like to take a brief but _____ swim.

Copyright © McDougal Littell/Houghton Mifflin Company.

CHAPTER 5

Lesson 1

What Is an Adjective?   *Application*

A. Writing Adjectives in Sentences

Use the word at the beginning of each item as an adjective in a sentence.

EXAMPLE silly *The silly story made us laugh.*

1. expensive _____

2. scary _____

3. nine _____

4. bright _____

5. Mexican _____

6. windy _____

7. slow _____

8. difficult _____

9. guilty _____

10. American _____

B. Writing a Paragraph Using Adjectives

Imagine a day at the beach. How would you describe the ocean or lake you are sitting near? What words could describe the people who are on the beach with you? Write a short paragraph about a day at the beach. Use at least five adjectives in your description. Underline the adjectives in your paragraph.

_____

_____

_____

_____

_____

_____

_____

_____

_____

Copyright © McDougal Littell/Houghton Mifflin Company.

Name _____ Date _____

Lesson 2 # Predicate Adjectives   *Teaching*

A **predicate adjective** is an adjective that follows a linking verb and describes the verb's subject. The linking verb connects the predicate adjective with the subject.

> The <u>flood</u> in spring <u>was</u> **disastrous.** (*disastrous* describes *flood*)

Often, forms of *be* are linking verbs, as in the above example. However, predicate adjectives can also follow other linking verbs, such as *taste, smell, feel, look, become,* and *seem*.

> Such a <u>calamity</u> <u>seemed</u> nearly **impossible.** (*impossible* describes *calamity*)

Identifying Predicate Adjectives

Underline the predicate adjective in each sentence. If the sentence has no predicate adjective, write **None** on the line to the right.

1. The valley in Johnstown, Pennsylvania, was very deep.   _____

2. The hills around Johnstown were high.   _____

3. The lake above Johnstown seemed unusually full.   _____

4. The concrete dam appeared weak.   _____

5. That day—May 31, 1889,—was stormy.   _____

6. The levels of the lake became dangerously high.   _____

7. Water rose almost to the top of the dam.   _____

8. The situation quickly became critical.   _____

9. Efforts to warn people were too late.   _____

10. When the dam broke, it sounded explosive.   _____

11. The flood waters were unstoppable.   _____

12. The flood destroyed everything in its path.   _____

13. The devastation of Johnstown was incredibly rapid.   _____

14. Once people heard of the disaster, they were generous to the victims. _____

15. The process of rebuilding Johnstown was slow.   _____

Copyright © McDougal Littell/Houghton Mifflin Company.

Lesson 2 Predicate Adjectives   *More Practice*

A. Identifying Predicate Adjectives and the Words They Modify

Underline the predicate adjective in each of the following sentences. Write the
word it modifies on the line to the right.

1. Swimmers should be careful of sharks.   _____

2. Puppies are helpless at birth.   _____

3. The space creature seemed friendly.   _____

4. The Apache fighters were resourceful.   _____

5. From the top of the skyscraper, the cars below look tiny. _____

6. After drinking the potion, Alice became very small.   _____

7. The spoiled milk tasted sour.   _____

8. Dorothy felt sorry for the scarecrow.   _____

9. The surface of Mars appears reddish.   _____

10. The tornado grew more powerful.   _____

B. Writing Predicate Adjectives

Complete each sentence with a predicate adjective. Write the predicate adjective
on the line.

1. The Johnstown Flood must have been _____.

2. People felt _____ when they saw the water rising.

3. The floodwaters must have sounded _____.

4. The lake was extremely _____.

5. The disaster seemed _____.

6. After the flood, people felt _____.

7. It was _____ to see the destruction.

8. The town looked _____.

9. The damage caused by the flood was _____.

10. The clean-up of the town must have been _____.

Copyright © McDougal Littell/Houghton Mifflin Company.

CHAPTER 5

Lesson 2

Predicate Adjectives

Application

A. Writing Predicate Adjectives in Sentences

Use the word at the beginning of each item as a predicate adjective in a sentence.

EXAMPLE creative *Artists are creative.*

1. proud _____

2. bright _____

3. spicy _____

4. unpleasant _____

5. impossible _____

6. unexpected _____

7. silly _____

8. difficult _____

9. empty _____

10. hot _____

B. Writing a Paragraph Using Predicate Adjectives

Imagine how it would have felt to have been a resident of Johnstown, Pennsylvania, on the night of the terrible flood. What might you have seen? How would you have felt? Write a short paragraph about your imagined experiences. Use at least four predicate adjectives in your description. Use a verb other than a form of be in at least two of the sentences. Underline the predicate adjectives in your paragraph.

_____

_____

_____

_____

_____

_____

_____

Copyright © McDougal Littell/Houghton Mifflin Company.

CHAPTER 5

Lesson 3 — Other Words Used as Adjectives

Teaching

Some nouns and pronouns can be used as adjectives. They can modify nouns.

Pronouns as Adjectives

This, that, these, and *those* are **demonstrative pronouns** that can be used as adjectives. *My, our, your, his, her, its,* and *their* are **possessive pronouns** that can be used as adjectives. **Indefinite pronouns** such as *all, each, both, few, many, most,* and *some* can be used as adjectives.

Demonstrative pronoun	Explorers searched for <u>that</u> tomb.
Possessive pronoun	They finally discovered <u>its</u> entrance.
Indefinite pronoun	They found <u>many</u> treasures.

Nouns as Adjectives Some nouns can be used as adjectives.

Noun	In the tomb was a necklace honoring the <u>sun</u> god.

Identifying Nouns and Pronouns Used as Adjectives

Underline the nouns or pronouns that are used as adjectives in each sentence.

1. A boy king named Tutankhamen ruled his land of Egypt for only a few years many centuries ago.
2. This pharaoh was only 18 at the time of his death.
3. When he was buried, his subjects surrounded him with many treasures.
4. At that time, all pharaohs of Egypt were buried with their favorite possessions, in case they would be needed in the afterlife.
5. Unfortunately, successors of Tutankhamen destroyed all monuments built in his honor.
6. All Egyptians forgot the location of his tomb.
7. In 1922, Howard Carter rediscovered this tomb.
8. This archaeologist had been searching for that site for many years.
9. Most people thought this discovery was spectacular.
10. Many royal tombs had been discovered, and their treasures had been stolen.
11. Luckily, few people had entered this tomb over the centuries.
12. A magnificent gold mask of Tutankhamen still covered the head and shoulders of his mummy.
13. In his tomb, those explorers also found many beautiful items including animal figures, ship models, and feather fans.
14. These items provided a picture of the daily lives of many ancient Egyptians.
15. Most items from this tomb are now in a Cairo museum.

Copyright © McDougal Littell/Houghton Mifflin Company.

CHAPTER 5

Name _____ Date _____

Lesson 3

Other Words Used as Adjectives

More Practice

A. Identifying Adjectives and the Words They Modify

Underline the pronouns or nouns used as adjectives in the following sentences.
Draw an arrow from the adjective to the word it modifies.

1. After hearing those weather reports, I think we should postpone our club picnic.

2. My favorite dessert is apple pie.

3. Some orchestra members need to tune their instruments.

4. Many loyal fans kept cheering for their baseball team.

5. That police captain spoke at our safety assembly.

6. Raul needs to buy some guitar strings.

7. Many customers prefer that camera.

8. We need these jars of tomato sauce for our spaghetti dinner.

9. Most pages in this photo album are filled.

10. Few snacks taste as good as your oatmeal cookies.

B. Writing Pronouns and Nouns Used as Adjectives

Complete each sentence with a noun or pronoun that is used as an adjective. Write
the adjective on the line.

1. Tutankhamen ruled _____ land 3,000 years ago.

2. Pharaohs were buried with _____ possessions.

3. People searched for Tutankhamen's tomb for _____ years.

4. The tomb was discovered with most of _____ treasures
untouched.

5. _____ people were amazed by these treasures.

6. _____ items are very valuable.

7. A _____ mask lay on top of Tutankhamen's mummy.

8. _____ discoveries impressed the world.

9. No one else has ever discovered a tomb as grand as _____ one.

10. Will the next amazing discovery be found in a _____ chest at the
bottom of the ocean?

Copyright © McDougal Littell/Houghton Mifflin Company.

Lesson 3 · **Other Words Used as Adjectives** · *Application*

A. Writing Adjectives in Sentences

Use the word at the beginning of each item as an adjective in a sentence.

EXAMPLE brick *A brick wall surrounded the estate.*

1. those _____

2. gold_____

3. bicycle _____

4. telephone _____

5. cement _____

6. cotton_____

7. several _____

8. our _____

9. most _____

10. their _____

B. Writing a Paragraph Using Pronouns and Nouns as Adjectives

Use at least four of the following nouns and pronouns as adjectives to describe the throne room of a royal palace. Write your paragraph on the lines below. Underline each of the listed words in your paragraph.

emerald	velvet	her	every
marble	his	that	some

_____

_____

_____

_____

_____

_____

_____

_____

_____

Copyright © McDougal Littell/Houghton Mifflin Company.

CHAPTER 5

Lesson 4

What Is an Adverb?

Teaching

An **adverb** is a word that modifies a verb, an adjective, or another adverb. Adverbs answer the questions *how, when, where,* or to *what extent.*

Modifying a verb	The fashion designer <u>skillfully</u> <u>sketches</u> her ideas.
Modifying an adjective	She is <u>always</u> <u>excited</u> about her shows.
Modifying an adverb	The seamstress sews <u>very</u> <u>well</u>.

Adverbs that modify adjectives or other adverbs usually come directly before the word they modify. They usually answer the question *To what extent?*

Adverbs	
How?	eagerly
When?	early
Where?	outside
To what extent?	totally

Many adverbs are formed by adding the suffix *-ly* to adjectives. Sometimes a base word's spelling changes whey *-ly* is added.

Adjective	bright	nimble	cozy
Adverb	bright<u>ly</u>	nim<u>bly</u>	cozi<u>ly</u>

Identifying Adverbs

Underline all the adverbs in each sentence. If there are no adverbs in a sentence, write **None** on the line to the right.

1. There is a big sale at the mall.   _____

2. People who shop wisely can save a great deal of money.   _____

3. Denice always goes to sales.   _____

4. In the past, she has been very lucky with her buys.   _____

5. She bought a rather expensive necklace very cheaply.   _____

6. She feels happy when she finds a real deal.   _____

7. For example, she once bought a nearly new tent at the outdoors store. _____

8. She will rather proudly show you the suitcase she bought for a dollar. _____

9. If you want a good deal, stay close to Deniece.   _____

10. She is amazingly skillful in spending and saving money.   _____

Copyright © McDougal Littell/Houghton Mifflin Company.

CHAPTER 5

Lesson 4

What Is an Adverb?

More Practice

A. Identifying Adverbs and the Words They Modify

Underline the adverbs in the following sentences. Draw an arrow from each adverb to the word it modifies.

1. Some settlers nearly died from hunger and cold.

2. The octopus silently wrapped its tentacles around its prey.

3. The *Challenger* suddenly exploded in midair.

4. Charles Goodyear accidentally dropped rubber onto a hot stove.

5. The superhero often uses her magic powers to capture villains.

6. People sleep outside under the stars.

7. Lincoln's Gettysburg Address lasted only two minutes.

8. Sacagawea guided the Lewis and Clark Expedition expertly.

9. The alien ship quickly flew to the distant planet.

10. The milk carton is almost empty.

B. Writing Adverbs

Complete each sentence with an adverb. Write the adverb on the line. [use theme]

1. The shopping mall was _____ busy the day Sean went shopping there.

2. _____ all the stores were filled with customers.

3. Sean _____ shops with a friend.

4. They _____ stop at the ice cream store in the center of the mall.

5. Sean and his friend were _____ surprised to see that the ice cream store was gone.

6. In its place was a _____ new store.

7. They stepped _____, and a clerk asked if she could help them.

8. They looked _____ and saw computer games on all the shelves.

9. As dedicated game players, the boys were _____ pleased with this new store.

10. On the other hand, where can they get a _____ good ice cream cone now?

Copyright © McDougal Littell/Houghton Mifflin Company.

CHAPTER 5

Lesson 4 What Is an Adverb?

Application

A. Writing Adverbs in Sentences

Use the adverb at the beginning of each item in a sentence.

EXAMPLE quietly *Janice quietly crept down the stairs.*

1. sadly _____

2. truthfully _____

3. extremely _____

4. rapidly_____

5. tomorrow _____

6. inside _____

7. seriously _____

8. almost _____

9. really _____

10. soon_____

B. Writing a Paragraph Using Adverbs

Choose four of the following adverbs to use in a paragraph about the career you would like to have when you grow up. Write the paragraph on the lines below. Underline each of these adverbs and any other adverb that you use in your paragraph.

eagerly	very	today	completely	usually
carefully	extremely	really	happily	someday

_____

_____

_____

_____

_____

_____

_____

_____

_____

Copyright © McDougal Littell/Houghton Mifflin Company.

CHAPTER 5

Making Comparisons

Lesson 5

Teaching

Adjectives and adverbs can be used to compare people or things. Special forms of these words are used to make comparisons.

Use the **comparative** form of an adjective or adverb when you compare a person or thing with one other person or thing. Use the **superlative** form of an adjective or adverb when you compare someone or something with more than one other person or thing.

Comparative	The Pacific Ocean is <u>larger</u> than the Atlantic Ocean.
Superlative	The Pacific Ocean is the <u>largest</u> ocean in the world.

For most **one-syllable** modifiers, add *-er* to form the comparative *(young, younger)* and *-est* to form the superlative *(old, oldest)*.

You can also add *-er* and *-est* to some **two-syllable** adjectives. With others, and with two-syllable adverbs, use the words more and most *(more careful, most calmly)*.

To form the comparative or superlative form of most modifiers with **three syllables,** use the words more and most *(more dangerous, most dangerous; more clumsily, most clumsily)*.

Be sure to use only one sign of comparison at a time. Do not use *-er* and *more* together. *(harder*, not *more harder)*.

The comparative and superlative forms of some adjectives and adverbs are formed in irregular ways: *good, better, best; bad, worse, worst; well, better, best; much, more, most; little, less, least.*

Identifying Comparative and Superlative Modifiers

On the line, label the boldfaced modifier **C** for comparative, or **S** for superlative.

1. Is the Indian Ocean **shallower** than the Atlantic Ocean? _____

2. The Pacific is the **deepest** of the oceans. _____

3. Tidal waves cause **worse** damage to the coastline than to the inland dunes. _____

4. A sea is **smaller** than an ocean. _____

5. The **longest** river in the world is the Nile in Africa. _____

6. Which river carries **more** water, the Nile or the Amazon? _____

7. Actually, the Amazon has the **most abundant** water supply of any river. _____

8. In many rivers, the water flows **more rapidly** near its source than close to its mouth. _____

9. Does the Mississippi River have **fewer** tributaries than the Missouri? _____

10. The **best** place to canoe on a river is away from sandbars and shallow areas. _____

Copyright © McDougal Littell/Houghton Mifflin Company.

Lesson 5 Making Comparisons

More Practice

A. Using Comparisons

Underline the correct form of comparison for each sentence.

1. Ocean currents are (more powerful, most powerful) than river currents.
2. The area of the ocean with the (warmer, warmest) water is found near the equator.
3. Mining for minerals in the ocean is (more expensive, most expensive) than land mining.
4. In long, narrow bays, tides are (higher, highest) than in other places.
5. Water pressure is (greater, greatest) on the ocean floor.
6. Unmanned submersibles can explore underwater wrecks (more safely, most safely) than divers can.
7. The fishing grounds in the North Sea are some of the (better, best) in the world.
8. Storms in the North Sea are (worse, worst) in the winter than at any other time.
9. Many people consider the Danube the (more beautiful, most beautiful) river in Europe.
10. The delta of the Niger River is the (larger, largest) delta in Africa.

B. Using Modifiers in Comparisons

After each sentence, write either the comparative or the superlative form of the word in parentheses, depending on what the sentence calls for.

1. That superhero is (fast) than lightning. _____

2. The wind started blowing (hard) as the storm approached. _____

3. Crocodiles are (small) than alligators. _____

4. They are (quick) than alligators too. _____

5. Jesse James was one of the (famous) outlaws in the Wild West. _____

6. The rain fell (steadily) than predicted. _____

7. Air pollution is (bad) in large cities than in most suburbs. _____

8. You can see that star (clearly) using a telescope. _____

9. African elephants are (large) than Indian elephants. _____

10. Did the tyrannosaurus fight its enemies (fiercely) than other dinosaurs? _____

11. Are the California redwoods the (old) living trees in the world? _____

12. You can carry that pack on your shoulders (easily) than in your hands. _____

Copyright © McDougal Littell/Houghton Mifflin Company.

CHAPTER 5

Making Comparisons

Application

A. Proofreading

Proofread the following paragraph. Look especially for comparison errors in adjectives and adverbs. If a sentence contains an error, rewrite the sentence correctly on the line with the same number. If it is correct, write **Correct** on the line.

How much do you know about the Great Lakes? **(1)** Do you realize that Lake Superior is the larger of the five lakes? **(2)** It is also the deepest. **(3)** Lake Erie lies most farthest south of all of the lakes. **(4)** Because Lake Erie is so shallow, its waves are more choppier than on any of the other lakes. **(5)** The smaller of all the Great Lakes is Lake Ontario. **(6)** Lake Michigan is the most biggest fresh water lake in the United States. **(7)** Except for Lake Superior, Lake Huron is greatest in size than the other Great Lakes.

1. _____

2. _____

3. _____

4. _____

5. _____

6. _____

7. _____

B. Using Comparisons in Writing

Picture an imaginary country, complete with lakes, rivers, oceans, and mountains. Give these natural features names. Then compare them to one another in a paragraph. In the paragraph, use the comparative or superlative forms at least five of the adjectives and adverbs below. Underline the forms you use.

tall	rapidly	safely	good	hard
deep	cold	brightly	bad	well
wide	warm	suddenly	strongly	little

_____

_____

_____

_____

_____

_____

Copyright © McDougal Littell/Houghton Mifflin Company.

Adjective or Adverb?   *Teaching*

Some pairs of adjectives and adverbs are often sources of confusion and mistakes.

Good or *Well*

Good is always an adjective; it modifies a noun or pronoun. *Well* is usually an adverb; it modifies a verb, adverb, or adjective. *Well* is an adjective when it refers to your health.

Adjective   That was a <u>good</u> meal. I felt <u>good</u> about it.
             I didn't feel <u>well</u> after I drank the spoiled milk.
Adverb   My father cooks <u>well</u>.

Real or *Really*

Real is always an adjective: it modifies a noun or pronoun. *Really* is always an adverb; it modifies a verb, adverb, or adjective.

Adjective   Dessert was a <u>real</u> treat.
Adverb   I was <u>really</u> hungry.

Bad or *Badly*

Bad is always an adjective: it modifies a noun or pronoun. *Badly* is always an adverb; it modifies a verb, adverb, or adjective.

Adjective   Those eggs smell <u>bad</u>.
Adverb   She burned the roast <u>badly</u>.

Using the Correct Adjective or Adverb

Underline the correct modifier from those given in parentheses.

1. One day, I decided to make a (real, really) fine dinner for my family.
2. Unfortunately, my stew turned out (bad, badly).
3. I was in a (real, really) hurry and forgot some of the ingredients.
4. I'm afraid I cooked the meat (bad, badly).
5. The stew both looked and smelled (bad, badly).
6. I decided I (real, really) wanted my mother to teach me how to cook.
7. My mother is a (good, well) cook.
8. I don't think she has made a (bad, badly) meal in her life.
9. We had a (good, well) time as she taught me.
10. I did my best to make a (real, really) good dinner.
11. I felt (good, well) when my family said they enjoyed it.
12. My family ate (good, well) that night.
13. I am happy to say that everyone in my family felt (good, well) after eating my meal.
14. I was proud of my first (real, really) success.
15. I think my Mom and I work (good, well) together.

Copyright © McDougal Littell/Houghton Mifflin Company.

CHAPTER 5

Lesson 6

Adjective or Adverb?

More Practice

A. Using the Correct Modifier

Underline the correct word in parentheses in each sentence. Label each word you choose as **ADJ** for adjective or **ADV** for adverb.

1. Cats can see (good, well) in the dark. _____

2. After the storm the pier was damaged (bad, badly). _____

3. I was (real, really) pleased to get your invitation. _____

4. Lila's medicine worked really (good, well) for her. _____

5. In the 1830s the Cherokees were treated very (bad, badly). _____

6. It was a (real, really) surprise to see my name on the list of winners. _____

7. The weather seemed too (bad, badly) to continue the game. _____

8. Sylvia looks (good, well) in her mermaid costume. _____

B. Writing with Adjectives and Adverbs

Decide if adjectives and adverbs are used correctly in the following sentences. If you find an error, rewrite the sentence correctly on the line. If the sentence is correct, write **Correct** on the line.

1. I wanted a snack real bad after I exercised.

_____

2. I needed a snack that was well for me.

_____

3. I could have had cheese and crackers, but that cheese smelled badly.

_____

4. Those cookies looked well, but I didn't think they were a real healthy snack.

_____

5. A lot of people like yogurt, but I think it tastes badly.

_____

6. I finally decided that fruit was a really good choice for me.

_____

Copyright © McDougal Littell/Houghton Mifflin Company.

CHAPTER 5

Lesson 6 Adjective or Adverb?   *Application*

A. Writing Sentences Using Adjectives and Adverbs Correctly

Write sentences using the adjectives and adverbs given.

1. good _____

2. well (adverb) _____

3. well (adjective) _____

4. bad _____

6. badly _____

7. real _____

8. really _____

B. Using Adjectives and Adverbs Correctly

Read the conversation below. It contains several errors in the use of *good, well, real, really, bad,* and *badly.* Underline any errors you find. Then rewrite the conversation correctly on the lines below.

"I feel real hungry, " said April. "I think I'm in the mood for some real good Italian food. Let's go to Marcello's Pizza Place."

"No thanks," replied Ross. "I think that pizza tastes badly. I'd rather have some real fine Chinese food."

"O.K. Chin's Restaurant makes sweet and sour pork real good. Do you suppose Justin is feeling well enough to come with us?"

"I'm afraid he is not doing good enough to go out to eat. His ankle still hurts bad."

"I feel badly that he can't join us, but let's go. I want to find out if Chin's food tastes as good as I remember."

_____

_____

_____

_____

_____

_____

_____

_____

Copyright © McDougal Littell/Houghton Mifflin Company.

CHAPTER 5

Lesson 7

Avoiding Double Negatives

Teaching

A **negative** is a word that means no.

Common Negative Words

barely	never	none	nothing	can't (cannot)
hardly	no	no one	nowhere	don't (do not)
neither	nobody	not	scarcely	hasn't (has not)

If two negative words are used where only one is needed, the result is a **double negative.** Avoid double negatives in your speaking and writing.

Nonstandard   My dog <u>hardly never</u> obeys me. (double negative)
Standard   My dog <u>hardly</u> ever obeys me.

A. Recognizing the Correct Use of Negatives

Circle the letter of the sentence from each pair that uses negatives correctly.

  1. a. June hasn't never had a pet.
     b. June hasn't ever had a pet.

  2. a. Nobody in our family wants a dog except me.
     b. Nobody in our family doesn't want a dog except me.

  3. a. My mother says she doesn't need no dog to take care of.
     b. My mother says she doesn't need any dog to take care of.

  4. a. I can't convince anybody that having a dog would be fun.
     b. I can't convince nobody that having a dog would be fun.

B. Avoiding Double Negatives

Underline the word in parentheses that correctly completes each sentence.

  1. We (couldn't, could) scarcely believe our eyes yesterday when we came home and found a cat in our house.

  2. No one had told (any, none) of us that we were getting a cat.

  3. My mother said, "We didn't want (either, neither) of you to know about this."

  4. My brothers and I clearly remember our dad saying, "We aren't (never, ever) going to have a pet in this household."

  5. Our dad didn't say (nothing, anything) to us when he changed his mind.

  6. He had seen the TV show about all those cats who didn't have (anywhere, nowhere) to live.

  7. Our cat was still in the animal shelter because she wasn't wanted by (nobody, anybody) else.

  8. Our parents couldn't have given us (no, any) better gift than our cat Jingles.

Copyright © McDougal Littell/Houghton Mifflin Company.

CHAPTER 5

Lesson 7 **Avoiding Double Negatives**   *More Practice*

A. Using Correct Modifiers

Underline the correct word in parentheses in each sentence.

1. Many explorers searched for gold but didn't find (any, none).
2. No one had seen (no, any) news of a spaceship landing in the desert.
3. Gerry couldn't believe that astronauts would (ever, never) go to Mars.
4. No one could do (anything, nothing) to control the robot's actions.
5. Elena hadn't (ever, never) heard the story about the headless horseman.
6. The stray puppy didn't have (anywhere, nowhere) to sleep.
7. My grandfather didn't watch (any, no) television until he was an adult.
8. Nothing you say (couldn't, could) make me change my mind.
9. My dog won't eat (none, any) of that dry dog food.

B. Avoiding Double Negatives

Rewrite each sentence to avoid double negatives. Some sentences can be corrected in more than one way.

1. A shepherd boy cried "Wolf" three times even though there wasn't no wolf.

   _____

2. Neighbors couldn't find a wolf nowhere.

   _____

3. Later, they didn't pay no attention to the shepherd boy's cries for help.

   _____

4. Since the wolf didn't have nothing to fear, it started attacking the sheep.

   _____

   _____

5. No one never believes a liar, even when he or she is telling the truth.

   _____

   _____

Copyright © McDougal Littell/Houghton Mifflin Company.

CHAPTER 5

Lesson 7   # Avoiding Double Negatives   *Application*

A. Avoiding Double Negatives

Choose one of these words to complete each sentence below. Be sure to avoid double negatives.

no	never	anyone	ever
anything	no one	barely	nothing

1. Our cat is so fat I can _____ pick her up.

2. I haven't _____ heard of anyone having a pig for a pet.

3. I didn't see _____ watching that dog in the park.

4. My sister has _____ nice to say about having a pet fish.

5. He can't teach his dog _____ unless he bribes him with food.

6. She can see _____ reason why you shouldn't get a hamster.

B. Revising a Paragraph with Double Negatives

The following paragraph contains several double negatives. Read each sentence and decide if it has a double negative. If it does, rewrite it correctly on the corresponding line below. If it is correct, write **Correct** on the corresponding line.

(1) When it comes to pet tricks, my cat isn't no star. **(2)** My dog, on the other hand, never stops surprising us with what he can learn. **(3)** We hadn't owned him for very long when he learned how to sit, lie down, and roll over. **(4)** Now you wouldn't hardly put him in the circus, but we think he is pretty fantastic. **(5)** Nobody couldn't believe how fast he learned how to catch a thrown stick. **(6)** If you put a dog bone on his nose, he can catch it in his mouth, and he hardly never drops it. **(7)** We couldn't scarcely believe it when he learned how to fetch our newspaper in the morning. **(8)** He loves attention, and he won't let no visitor leave our house without showing that person one of his special tricks.

1. _____

2. _____

3. _____

4. _____

5. _____

6. _____

7. _____

8. _____

CHAPTER 5

Copyright © McDougal Littell/Houghton Mifflin Company.

Lesson 1

What Is a Preposition?

Teaching

A **preposition** is a word that shows a relationship between a noun or pronoun and some other word in the sentence.

> The girls are playing <u>in</u> the yard. (*in* shows the relationship between *girls* and *yard*)

Common Prepositions				
about	at	despite	like	to
above	before	down	near	toward
across	behind	during	of	under
after	below	except	off	until
against	beneath	for	on	up
along	beside	from	out	with
among	between	in	over	within
around	beyond	inside	past	without
as	by	into	through	

A **prepositional phrase** consists of a preposition, its object, and any modifiers of the object. The **object of the preposition** is the noun or pronoun following the preposition.

> Rome is the capital <u>of</u> Italy. (The preposition is *of*, the object of the preposition is *Italy*, and the prepositional phrase is *of Italy*.)

Sometimes the same word can be used as a preposition or as an adverb. If the word has no object, it is an adverb.

> **Adverb** We spent the afternoon walking <u>around</u>. (no object)
> **Preposition** We walked <u>around</u> the city streets. (object = *streets*)

A. Finding Prepositions and Their Objects

Underline the preposition in each sentence. Underline the object or objects of the preposition twice.

1. The plane finally landed in Rome.

2. I had actually reached the city of my dreams.

3. I gazed out the window as we taxied closer.

4. Was that the Coliseum I saw to the right?

5. I imagined Julius Caesar marching with his troops.

6. During the next few days, I would explore the city.

B. Recognizing Prepositions and Adverbs

Decide whether the boldfaced word is a preposition or an adverb. Write **P** on the line if it is a preposition. Write **A** if it is an adverb.

1. I could barely see **through** the window because it was steamed up. _____

2. Let us drive **through,** please. _____

3. Turn the light **on** before you enter the room. _____

4. Write your name **on** the top line. _____

Copyright © McDougal Littell/Houghton Mifflin Company.

CHAPTER 6

Lesson 1 ## What Is a Preposition?   *More Practice*

A. Identifying Prepositions and Their Objects

Underline each preposition once. Circle the object of the preposition. Sentences may have more than one prepositional phrase.

1. A tugboat pushes barges down the river.

2. The pinch hitter drove the ball deep into left field.

3. The Sioux people depended greatly on the buffalo.

4. Dr. Frankenstein conducted amazing experiments in his laboratory.

5. Native Americans make moccasins from dried animal skins.

6. The word *pajamas* comes from the Persian language.

7. Treasure hunters found gold off the coast of Florida.

8. The detective examined the fingerprints through his magnifying glass.

9. The jets disappeared behind the clouds.

10. In the morning, a bird sings outside my window.

B. Writing with Prepositional Phrases

Underline the prepositional phrase in each sentence. Then replace that phrase with a different prepositional phrase, and write your new sentence on the line. Be sure to use a different preposition and a new object of the preposition.

EXAMPLE Our hotel is across the river.
Our hotel is behind the clock tower.

1. The cab drove around the block.

   _____

2. Visitors are fascinated by the ancient ruins.

   _____

3. Gardens bloom on sunny hillsides.

   _____

4. The church was built during the 1500s.

   _____

5. A famous art museum is in the old palace.

   _____

6. Throw a coin into the fountain.

   _____

Copyright © McDougal Littell/Houghton Mifflin Company.

CHAPTER 6

What Is a Preposition?

Application

A. Writing with Prepositional Phrases

Add one or more prepositional phrases to each simple sentence. Write your new sentence on the line.

1. The soldiers marched.

_____

2. The emperor spoke.

_____

3. The athletes competed.

_____

4. The wise men taught.

_____

5. The frightened people hid.

_____

B. Writing with Prepositional Phrases

Use three of these prepositional phrases in an original story. Write your story on the lines below. Underline the phrases from the list that you use in your story.

by the stadium	under the ground	without a reason
after the game	above the sign	inside the elegant home
in the stands	over the fence	until morning

_____

_____

_____

_____

_____

_____

_____

_____

_____

_____

Copyright © McDougal Littell/Houghton Mifflin Company.

CHAPTER 6

Lesson 2 Using Prepositional Phrases

Teaching

A **prepositional phrase** is always related to another word in a sentence. It modifies the word in the same way an adjective or adverb does.

An **adjective phrase** is a prepositional phrase that modifies a noun or a pronoun. It can tell *which one, how many,* or *what kind.*

> The trees <u>on the mountain top</u> were spindly. (The phrase *on the mountain top* modifies the noun *trees.*)

An **adverb phrase** is a prepositional phrase that modifies a verb, an adjective, or another adverb. It usually tells *where, when, how, why,* or *to what extent.*

Modifying a verb	The hikers stayed <u>on the trail</u>. (The phrase *on the trail* modifies the verb *stayed.*)
Modifying an adjective	Our bodies felt heavy <u>with fatigue</u>. (The phrase *with fatigue* modifies the adjective *heavy.*)
Modifying an adverb	My grandmother hiked well <u>for her age</u>. (The phrase *for her age* modifies the adverb *well.*)

Placement of Prepositional Phrases Place the prepositional phrase close to the word it modifies, or else you may confuse your readers.

Confusing	<u>With four babies,</u> we surprised a mother <u>bird</u>.
Better	We surprised a mother <u>bird</u> <u>with four babies.</u>

Identifying Prepositional Phrases

Underline the prepositional phrase in each sentence. If it is an adjective phrase, write **ADJ** on the line to the right. If it is an adverb phrase, write **ADV.**

1. Last summer our whole family hiked up a mountain. _____

2. From the beginning the trail was rocky and steep. _____

3. Hiking shoes with tough soles were absolutely necessary. _____

4. The trail led us up a steep rise. _____

5. On one side was a rocky ledge. _____

6. The view from the other side was fantastic. _____

7. The other mountains across the valley looked beautiful too. _____

8. My dad carried a camera around his neck. _____

9. We stopped along the way to take pictures. _____

10. After a while we got pretty hungry and ate lunch. _____

11. The trip down the mountain was easier than the trip up. _____

Copyright © McDougal Littell/Houghton Mifflin Company.

CHAPTER 6

Lesson 2 **Using Prepositional Phrases** *More Practice*

A. Identifying Prepositional Phrases

In each sentence, underline the word modified by the boldfaced prepositional phrase. On the blank, write **ADJ** or **ADV** to identify what kind of prepositional phrase it is.

1. Please wait **outside the front door.**   _____

2. The rug **under your feet** came from Persia many years ago.   _____

3. The valley **between the mountains** was green and lush.   _____

4. Some people always sit **near the end** of the row in a theater.   _____

5. **On a warm summer day,** this river is filled with canoes.   _____

6. The door **beside the water fountai**n leads to the cafeteria.   _____

7. How long can you live **without oxygen?**   _____

8. I can make a walkie-talkie **with two empty cans.**   _____

9. I bought a book **of stamps** at the post office.   _____

10. Read us the story **about the puppet** who became a real boy.   _____

B. Placing Prepositional Phrases

Rewrite each sentence, changing the position of one or more prepositional phrases so that the sentence is no longer confusing.

> **EXAMPLE** The trip was hard for the hikers up the mountain.
> *The trip up the mountain was hard for the hikers.*

1. In their backpacks the hikers ate the sandwiches.

_____

2. With cheeks filled with nuts, they met a squirrel.

_____

3. One hiker inside a hollow log saw a chipmunk run.

_____

4. A hiker on one of the highest branches of a tree spotted an eagle.

_____

Copyright © McDougal Littell/Houghton Mifflin Company.

CHAPTER 6

Lesson
2

Using Prepositional Phrases *Application*

A. Revising Sentences with Misplaced Prepositional Phrases

Rewrite each sentence, changing the position of one or more prepositional phrases so that the sentence is no longer confusing.

EXAMPLE On a star Janice made a wish.
Janice made a wish on a star.

1. We sat down for a lunch in the park of ham sandwiches.

_____

2. We passed a girl on a bicycle with long hair.

_____

3. The wastebasket spilled its contents next to my jacket of garbage.

_____

4. Valerie told us about the strange dream she had at breakfast.

_____

5. The waiter brought the ice cream to the customer with chocolate syrup.

_____

B. Using Prepositional Phrases as Adjectives and Adverbs

Add a prepositional phrase to each sentence. The type of phrase to add is indicated in parentheses after the sentence.

1. The hike was fun. (Add an adjective phrase.)

_____

2. The wind was blowing. (Add an adverb phrase.)

_____

3. I saw an eagle fly. (Add an adverb phrase.)

_____

4. A fallen tree blocked the trail. (Add an adjective phrase.)

_____

5. My friend and I sat on a big rock. (Add an adjective phrase.)

_____

CHAPTER 6

Copyright © McDougal Littell/Houghton Mifflin Company.

Copyright © McDougal Littell/Houghton Mifflin Company.

Lesson 3 Conjunctions   *Teaching*

A **conjunction** is a word used to join words or groups of words. Different kinds of conjunctions do different jobs.

Conjunctions connect words used in the same way. The words joined by a conjunction can be subjects, predicates, or any other kind of sentence part.

Some common coordinating conjunctions are *and, but, or,* and *nor.*

Use *and* to connect similar things or ideas. Use *but* to contrast things or ideas. Use *or* and *nor* to show choices.

> Yesterday, I went to the amusement park <u>and</u> rode the roller coaster.
> The park was crowded <u>but</u> fun.
> The roller coaster <u>or</u> the Ferris wheel may be my favorite ride.

Conjunctions can also join whole thoughts, such as two sentences that are closely related. Use a comma before the conjunction when joining two sentences.

> I got into line, <u>and</u> I waited for about 30 minutes.
> The wait was really long, <u>but</u> the ride was definitely worth it.

Identifying Conjunctions

Underline all the conjunctions in the following sentences.

1. When we went to the amusement park, we came in the morning and stayed until after dark.
2. The Ferris wheel used to frighten me, but now I like it.
3. The Flying Turns and the Tower of Terror are other good rides.
4. My friend Steve or my brother Tom went on the roller coaster with me.
5. Steve doesn't like the popcorn balls at the park, nor do I.
6. I used to like the kiddie rides, but now they seem boring.
7. The roller coaster carries riders up and down so quickly!
8. Do you prefer the stand-up coasters or the inverted coasters?
9. Sometimes the ride turns you upside down, and sometimes you become airborne.
10. The ride twists and turns in the middle.
11. Do you like to sit at the front or the back on a roller coaster?
12. If you sit in the front, you get a great view, and you can see what's coming first.
13. If you sit in the back, the ride seems faster and scarier.
14. Would you rather ride the roller coaster again or try a different ride?
15. The merry-go-round doesn't have a long line, nor does the antique car ride.
16. My parents don't ride the roller coaster very often, but I will enjoy it even when I'm old.

CHAPTER 6

Lesson 3 # Conjunctions

More Practice

A. Identifying Conjunctions

In the following sentences, underline the conjunctions.

1. Would you rather go to the beach or spend the day at an amusement park?
2. Amusement parks provide fun and relaxation for people of all ages.
3. Some people enjoy the rides, and other like the live shows.
4. You don't think about your worries while you are there, nor are you held to your daily routines.
5. At some parks, you can eat at a restaurant or enjoy a picnic lunch.
6. Do you like popcorn balls, or do you prefer salt water taffy?
7. You get wet on this ride, but it is fun anyway.
8. The merry-go-round is an old ride, but it is still one of the most popular rides.
9. Hold on tight, and scream all the way down on the roller coaster!
10. Some people say that roller coasters go too fast and are too dangerous, but I really enjoy them.

B. Using Conjunctions

Complete each of the following sentences with a conjunction.

EXAMPLE Her clothes were worn, _____*but*_____ they were clean and neat.

1. On the merry-go-round you can ride a horse _____ you can ride a lion.

2. The Confederate troops won many battles, _____ the Union troops won the war.

3. At the history museum, a log cabin _____ an old locomotive were on display.

4. The paper airplane climbed steeply _____ then dived toward the ground.

5. Do you want French toast _____ scrambled eggs for breakfast?

6. Food isn't allowed in this store, _____ are drinks.

7. I looked for my flashlight, _____ it wasn't in its regular place.

8. The day was cold _____ pleasant for this time of year.

9. At the grocery store I bought milk, eggs, _____ bread.

10. This restaurant doesn't offer hamburgers _____ cheeseburgers.

Copyright © McDougal Littell/Houghton Mifflin Company.

CHAPTER 6

Lesson 3 Conjunctions

Application

A. Proofreading

Proofread the following paragraph, adding appropriate conjunctions where they are needed.

Ask most people _____ they will say that the best ride in the amusement park is the roller coaster. In the past, there was really only one kind of roller coaster—the wooden one where you sat in a car and rode up _____ down a series of hills—_____ now there are other kinds to choose from. In a stand-up coaster, you don't sit down at all, _____ you stand up _____ are strapped in. You ride up and down _____ do loop-the-loops. In an inverted coaster, you ride upside down below the tracks, _____ in a hypercoaster you go incredibly fast. After you ride a coaster you may feel great, _____ you may feel sick. If you feel great, it is because your adrenaline has kicked in. If you feel sick, your body can't keep up with the excitement. When that happens, just sit down _____ close your eyes, _____ you will feel like trying the coaster again very soon.

B. Writing with Conjunctions

Imagine a day at an amusement park. Write a diary entry about what you would do, see, or eat there. Use at least three different conjunctions in your entry. Underline every conjunction that you use.

_____

_____

_____

_____

_____

_____

_____

_____

_____

_____

Copyright © McDougal Littell/Houghton Mifflin Company.

Lesson 4 Interjections   *Teaching*

An **interjection** is a word or short phrase used to express emotion, such as *wow* and *my goodness.*

> Boy, that was a high jump!
> Hey! How can she run so fast?

Identifying Interjections

Read each sentence. If it contains an interjection, write the interjection on the line to the right. If it does not contain an interjection, write **None** on the line.

1. Excellent! We have tickets to the regional track meet! _____

2. Hey, aren't we supposed to go this way to our seats? _____

3. I don't know who is competing in this race. Do you? _____

4. Ick! Do they call this pizza? _____

5. Heavens! The crowd here is huge! _____

6. Ouch! Somebody just stepped on my foot. _____

7. Finally, here we are at our seats. _____

8. Quick, which race is starting now? _____

9. Wow! Look at those runners go! _____

10. Gosh, those two runners seemed to cross the finish line together. _____

11. Which runner will be awarded the prize? _____

12. Fantastic! The one from our high school has won! _____

13. When does the stadium close? Is it soon? _____

14. Great! We can stay for a about two more hours. _____

15. The athletes who compete here practice every day for hours. Amazing! _____

16. Okay, which event comes next? _____

17. The runners are lining up at the starting line. _____

18. Zoom! There they go! _____

Copyright © McDougal Littell/Houghton Mifflin Company.

CHAPTER 6

Lesson 4 **Interjections**   *More Practice*

A. Identifying Interjections

Read each sentence. If it contains an interjection, write the interjection on the line to the right. If it does not contain an interjection, write **None** on the line.

1. Say, isn't today your sister's birthday?   _____

2. Gosh! You're right!   _____

3. It's a good thing I bought her a present a month ago.   _____

4. Now, where did I put that gift?   _____

5. Unbelievable! I know I left the box in the closet, but now it's missing!   _____

6. Calm down, Cindy. You'll find it.   _____

7. Hooray! Here it is under my bed!   _____

8. Why, I thought you had forgotten my birthday.   _____

9. Ridiculous! Who could forget something so important?   _____

10. We hope you have a happy birthday and a great year!   _____

B. Using Interjections

Write a different interjection before each of these sentences.

EXAMPLE _____*Hooray!*_____ Our team won the championship!

1. _____, who is singing that song on the radio?

2. _____! The bus is leaving! Let's run for it!

3. _____! We lost the game!

4. _____! That was an excellent performance.

5. _____! These French fries are cold!

6. _____! I though that ball was uncatchable!

7. _____! It's really cold today!

8. _____, this is the first time I ever played handball.

9. _____! You closed the door on my hand!

10. _____! That's my sweatshirt, not yours!

Copyright © McDougal Littell/Houghton Mifflin Company.

CHAPTER 6

Lesson 4 Interjections   *Application*

A. Writing Sentences with Interjections

Write a sentence for each of these interjections. Decide whether to use a comma
or an exclamation point after the interjection. An exclamation point after an
interjection shows stronger emotion than a comma does.

> **EXAMPLE** Wow *Wow! You're really good at this game!*

1. hey _____

2. no _____

3. hooray _____

4. ick _____

5. awesome _____

6. ow _____

7. excellent _____

8. yuck _____

9. yikes _____

10. well _____

B. Writing a Letter with Interjections

Write a letter to a friend describing an event you saw at a summer or winter
Olympics. At the Summer Games, you would see track and field events, swimming,
basketball, archery, bicycling, gymnastics, and weight lifting. At the Winter Games,
you might see bobsledding, figure skating, ice hockey, skiing, luge, or speed skating.
Use at least four interjections, for whenever you want to express emotion.

_____

_____

_____

_____

_____

_____

_____

_____

CHAPTER 6

Copyright © McDougal Littell/Houghton Mifflin Company.

Lesson 1

Agreement in Number

Teaching

A verb must agree with its subject in number. **Number** refers to whether a word is singular—naming one—or plural—naming more than one.

A singular subject takes a singular verb.

> That **poster** <u>announces</u> a garage sale. (singular subject, singular verb)

A plural subject takes a plural verb.

> Those **posters** <u>announce</u> garage sales. (plural subject, plural verb)

In a sentence with a verb phrase, the first helping verb must agree with the subject.

> The **neighbors** <u>have</u> been joining in an annual **sale**.

The **contractions** doesn't and don't are short forms of *does not* and *do not*. Use *doesn't* with all singular subjects except *I* and *you*. Use *don't* with all plural subjects, *I,* and *you.*

> <u>Does</u>n't your **neighborhood** <u>have</u> sales? <u>Don</u>'t your **neighbors** <u>like</u> sales?

Making Subjects and Verbs Agree in Number

In each sentence, underline the subject. Then underline the verb in parentheses that agrees with the subject.

1. The bicycle (was, were) not for sale.
2. Marie always (look, looks) for mystery novels.
3. Her father (want, wants) to find old hand tools.
4. The newspaper (include, includes) ads for garage sales.
5. The ads (list, lists) some of the things for sale.
6. The sellers (were, was) still marking prices when the first customers came.
7. (Don't, Doesn't) Marc want to go to the sale?
8. (Has, Have) Ashley ever bought anything here?
9. I (am, are) looking for old vinyl records.
10. We (haven't, hasn't) found any hardcover books.

B. Identifying Subjects and Verbs That Agree in Number

In each sentence, underline the subject and the verb. On the line following the sentence, write whether the two parts of the sentence **Agree** or **Disagree** in number.

1. Several coyotes has been spotted in the park. _____

2. The kite rises easily in this wind. _____

3. You has worn my boots! _____

4. The mail has arrived already. _____

5. Most drivers obeys the traffic rules. _____

Copyright © McDougal Littell/Houghton Mifflin Company.

CHAPTER 7

Agreement in Number

More Practice

A. Making Subjects and Verbs Agree in Number

On the line following each sentence, write the present tense form of the verb to agree with the subject.

1. Every summer, my friends and I (go) to garage sales. _____

2. As usual, today Maria (be) looking for a cup to replace the one she broke. _____

3. One antique dealer always (arrive) at a sale an hour early. _____

4. The music teacher (look) for old sheet music at a house sale. _____

5. John (want) to find hockey equipment at a yard sale. _____

6. Anna (find) the neatest old clothes at garage sales. _____

7. Usually, she (buy) at least one or two floppy hats. _____

8. James and Gary (hope) to find a good used bike for their little sister. _____

9. I (be) one of the ones who arrived at the sale late. _____

10. Martha (say) she will look but won't buy anything. _____

B. Correcting Agreement Errors

In each sentence, underline both the subject and the verb. If the verb agrees with the subject, write **Correct** on the line at the right. If it does not agree, write the correct verb.

1. Carl sing in his church choir. _____

2. The captain stand at the wheel of the ship. _____

3. Marsha and Kelley sit together in the cafeteria. _____

4. Jon was asking about used bicycles. _____

6. Mr. Adams have been working here for 12 years. _____

7. Whoops! The bucket are overflowing. _____

8. My parents insist on no TV at dinnertime. _____

9. The cats was watching the birds outside the window. _____

10. Marie has found a dollar bill on the sidewalk. _____

Copyright © McDougal Littell/Houghton Mifflin Company.

Agreement in Number

Lesson 1

Application

A. Proofreading for Errors in Agreement

Underline the five verbs in this paragraph that do not agree with their subjects. On the lines below, write the numbers of the sentences in which you find agreement errors. After each sentence number, write the subject and the verb form that agrees with it.

(1) Aunt Emma can't pass up garage sales. **(2)** She get a lot of clothes at them. **(3)** Some skirts and blouses is old enough to be back in style. **(4)** The clothing is usually in pretty good shape. **(5)** At a garage sale, the best thing are the prices. **(6)** Aunt Emma often change her mind. **(7)** Sometimes she wears a skirt only once or twice. **(8)** After that, she thinks it isn't right for her. **(9)** Then she don't want it any more. **(10)** She doesn't feel so bad about getting rid of outfits worth only a dollar or two.

_____

_____

_____

_____

B. Making Subjects and Verb Agree in Writing

Choose one of the topics below and write a paragraph of at least four sentences about it. Use the present tense throughout. Make sure the subjects and verbs of all the sentences agree.

_____

_____

_____

_____

_____

_____

_____

Trading cards	Recycling toys and games
A little store I like	Used book stores
What to do with old clothes	Selling old sports equipment
Costume parties	House or garage sales

Copyright © McDougal Littell/Houghton Mifflin Company.

CHAPTER 7

Lesson 2 · Compound Subjects   *Teaching*

A **compound subject** is made up of two or more simple subjects joined by a conjunction such as *and, or,* or *nor.*

And A compound subject whose subjects are joined by *and* usually takes a plural verb.

The <u>dog</u> **and** the <u>horse</u> <u>have been</u> important to humans for centuries.

Or or Nor When the parts of a compound subject are joined by *or* or *nor,* the verb should agree with the part closest to it.

Either the still <u>photos</u> **or** the <u>video</u> <u>shows</u> the lion's mane.
Neither the <u>spider</u> **nor** the <u>centipede</u> <u>is</u> an insect.

Making Verbs Agree with Compound Subjects

In each sentence, underline each part of the compound subject. Underline twice the word joining the parts. Then underline the verb in parentheses that agrees with the subject.

1. Either the wild dogs or the baboon (makes, make) that howling sound.
2. Neither crackers nor bread (is, are) good for the ducks.
3. The tourists and their guide (waits, wait) tensely for the elephant to cross the road.
4. Neither the tourists nor their guide (has, have) time to photograph the gazelle.
5. Either the salt lick or the acorns (attracts, attract) the deer to this spot.
6. Both the zoo director and his assistants (speaks, speak) at fundraisers.
7. Neither the drivers nor the pedestrian with a boom box (hears, hear) the birds.
8. Either the deer or the beavers (has, have) been eating the small saplings.
9. Neither the library filmstrips nor the TV documentary (mentions, mention) the mongoose.
10. The collie and the sheepdog (is, are) both from Europe.
11. In many folktales, either wolves or a wicked stepmother (threatens, threaten) the children.
12. Neither the skunk nor the dogs (wants, want) to see each other.
13. Among reindeer, both the male and the female (grows, grow) antlers.
14. Neither my spaniel nor my neighbor's terriers (does, do) tricks.
15. Bug bites or a bee sting (causes, cause) allergic reactions in some people.
16. The squirrels and the pigeons (competes, compete) for the bird seed that my neighbor puts out.

Copyright © McDougal Littell/Houghton Mifflin Company.

Name _____ Date _____

Compound Subjects

More Practice

A. Making Verbs Agree with Compound Subjects

In each sentence, underline each part of the compound subject. Underline twice the word joining the parts. Then underline the verb in parentheses that agrees with the subject.

1. Neither the senators nor the President (is, are) coming to the ceremony.
2. Either sugar or honey (is, are) acceptable, according to the recipe.
3. Both the graduate and his family (was, were) mentioned in the newspaper article.
4. Either the runners or the walkers (has, have) trampled the flower bed.
5. Neither the mayor nor her aides (is, are) available to answer our questions.
6. Neither the old jeans nor the new shirt (fits, fit) me.
7. Books and lunches (was, were) strewn all over the room.
8. Neither Vermonters nor New Yorkers (want, wants) Lake Champlain polluted.
9. Either my science project or my shoes (is, are) in that bag.
10. Both the bikes and the car (fits, fit) in the garage, but only with careful placement.

B. Using the Correct Verb with a Compound Subject

Write the correct present-tense form of the given verb. Make it agree with the compound subject.

1. Either the bird swings or the small bell (cost) two dollars. _____
2. Dad or my uncles (have) the framed photo of their family dog. _____
3. Unlike lions, neither tigers nor cheetahs (live) in groups. _____
4. Both the polar bear and the caribou (survive) in the Arctic. _____
5. Neither the ducks nor the fox (is, are) entirely believable in the story. _____
6. Either a raccoon or mice (disturb) our garbage every garbage-pickup day. _____
7. Neither hunters nor city sprawl (limit) the deer population. _____
8. Either Dr. Donnelly or her assistants (examine) the new animals at the zoo. _____
9. Neither birds nor the platypus (give) birth to live babies. _____
10. Several turtles and a lizard (crawl) onto the sunny spot on the rock. _____

Copyright © McDougal Littell/Houghton Mifflin Company.

CHAPTER 7

Compound Subjects

Lesson 2

Application

A. Correcting Errors in Agreement

Find the mistakes in the paragraph. For each sentence, write the correct present tense verb to agree with the subject. If the verb does agree, write **Correct.**

(1) Children and adults enjoy a pet's company. (2) Neither dangerous animals nor any wild animal are a good choice for a pet. (3) Both love and a caring attitude is requirements for pet ownership. (4) Either a hamster or a turtle makes a good pet for a small apartment. (5) Kittens and puppies is available for adoption at shelters.

1. _____

2. _____

3. _____

4. _____

5. _____

B. Using the Correct Verb with Compound Subjects

Write a sentence using each compound subject given in parentheses. Add words to the given subject as needed for the sense of the sentence.

1. (this mare and her foal) _____

_____

2. (many goldfish or one larger fish) _____

_____

3. (neither untrained puppies nor a frisky older dog)

_____

_____

4. (either a park or open fields)

_____

5. (either a dog-walker or neighbor children)

_____

6. (neither Sarah's parents nor her brother)

_____

Copyright © McDougal Littell/Houghton Mifflin Company.

CHAPTER 7

Lesson 3   Phrases Between Subject and Verbs   *Teaching*

Many errors in subject-verb agreement occur when a prepositional phrase falls between the subject and verb.

The subject of a verb is never part of a prepositional phrase. Mentally block out any words between the subject and verb. Make the verb agree with the subject.

> This **photo** of trees and flowers **wins** first prize. (singular subject and verb)
> The **trees** in the photo **are** stately. (plural subject and verb)

A. Making Subjects and Verbs Agree

Underline the subject of each sentence. Draw a line through any phrase that separates the subject from the verb. Finally, underline the verb in parentheses that agrees with the subject.

1. The view of the lawns and gardens (was, were) breathtaking.
2. One huge tree with the red and yellow leaves (is, are) in the background.
3. The trees in the orchard (provide, provides) apples for pies and cobblers.
4. A house with the white-trimmed windows (is, are) at the top of the hill.
5. The days of autumn (thrills, thrill) me every year.
6. Hours of raking and other cleanup work (pays, pay) off in the spring.
7. A lawn under a carpet of red and golden leaves (reminds, remind) me of my bed covered with a warm blanket.
8. The city park, in the opinion of many residents, (is, are) at its best in fall

B. Making Subjects and Verbs Agree

Underline the subject of each sentence. Draw a line through any phrase that separates the subject from the verb. Then write the form of the verb in parentheses that agrees with the subject.

1. Marie, in a heavy parka and waterproof hiking boots, (love) walking in the woods in winter.   _____

2. Books with the author's signature (be) worth more.   _____

3. A clown with three dogs in a wagon (be) leading the parade.   _____

4. Tall frameworks of iron (support) skyscrapers.   _____

5. Artists of that group (lead) the way toward a new style.   _____

6. Slippers of glass, in reality, (be) not very useful.   _____

7. A paper with more than six erasures (receive) a lower grade.   _____

8. The fourth book in that series (have) the strongest plot of all. _____

Copyright © McDougal Littell/Houghton Mifflin Company.

CHAPTER

Phrases Between Subject and Verbs

Lesson 3

More Practice

A. Making Subjects and Verbs Agree

Underline the subject. Then underline the verb that agrees with the subject.

1. The thought of so many cars on the roads (scare, scares) me.
2. The bridges across the winding river (connects, connect) different sections of the city.
3. The woman with the three children (need, needs) a babysitter tonight.
4. The strawflowers for sale at the market (make, makes) a pretty wreath.
5. Dinners at this time of year (seems, seem) incomplete without pumpkin pie.
6. A hayride under the stars (provides, provide) an evening of fun.
7. Legends of a monster in the swamp (has, have) frightened children in this region for generations.
8. Ann and Isaiah, with all their relatives at the seashore, (plays, play) a wild game of volleyball.
9. The parade of ghosts and goblins (comes, come) down our street.
10. One package of candies (isn't, aren't) enough.
11. Those dishes of fine china (makes, make) me nervous.
12. Only one of these problems (has, have) to be solved right now.

B. Correcting Agreement in Number

In each of these sentences, decide whether the verb agrees with the subject. If it does, write **Correct** on the line. If it does not, write the correct form of the verb on the line.

1. Two nests on the windowsills of the office building holds eggs. _____

2. The painting full of wild animals appeals to him. _____

3. The clown with the orange hair and big shoes make me laugh. _____

4. The men in the dragon float is in the parade every year. _____

5. The enormous string of beads were my idea. _____

6. A bouquet of flowers go to the winner. _____

7. In the fall, a pile of leaves is fun to jump into. _____

8. The cage with the monkeys always attract a crowd. _____

9. The people in the house on the corner is giving out candy bars. _____

10. A traveling carnival with all sorts of rides pass inspection every year. _____

Copyright © McDougal Littell/Houghton Mifflin Company.

CHAPTER 7

Phrases Between Subject and Verbs

Lesson 3

Application

A. Correcting Agreement in Number

Underline the subject and verb of each numbered sentence. If there is an agreement error, write the subject and the correct form of the verb on the lines below. If the subject and verb agree, write **Correct.**

(1) One of my favorite fall activities are hiking in the woods. (2) The fallen leaves, like a warm blanket over the cold earth, rustle softly under my feet. (3) The path through the woods follow the course of a small stream. (4) The murmurs of the stream creates nature's sound effects especially for me. (5) A friend along with you make the experience even better.

1. _____

2. _____

3. _____

4. _____

5. _____

B. Making Subjects and Verbs Agree

In each sentence beginning below, underline the word that should be used as the simple subject in a sentence. Then supply a complete predicate, including a verb of your choice, to complete the sentence. Make sure your verb agrees with the underlined subject.

EXAMPLE The girls on the swimming team *eat lunch together.*

1. The cost of stamps

_____

2. The cooks in the restaurant

_____

3. The cage with the hamsters

_____

4. The slices of pizza

_____

5. The pages of the book

_____

Copyright © McDougal Littell/Houghton Mifflin Company.

Copyright © McDougal Littell/Houghton Mifflin Company.

Lesson 4

Indefinite Pronoun Subjects

Teaching

An **indefinite pronoun** does not refer to a definite, or specific, person, place, thing, or idea.

When used as subjects, some indefinite pronouns are always singular. Others are always plural. Others can be singular or plural depending on how they are used.

Indefinite Pronouns					
Always Singular	another	each	everything	nothing	something
	anybody	either	neither	one	
	anyone	everybody	nobody	somebody	
	anything	everyone	no one	someone	
Always Plural	both	few	many	several	
Singular or Plural	all	any	most	none	some

Singular indefinite pronouns take singular verbs.

> <u>Everybody</u> <u>likes</u> good food.

Plural indefinite pronouns take plural verbs.

> <u>Many</u> <u>like</u> hot, spicy food.

All, any, most, none, and *some* can be singular or plural. If the pronoun refers to a single person or thing, it takes a singular verb. If it refers to more than one person or thing, it takes a plural verb.

> <u>All</u> of the hamburgers <u>were</u> eaten. (more than one hamburger was eaten)

> <u>All</u> of the hamburger <u>was</u> eaten. (hamburger is considered a unit)

Making Indefinite Pronouns and Verbs Agree

In each sentence, underline the indefinite pronoun used as subject and the verb. (If a verb includes more than one word, underline only the first helping verb.) If the verb agrees with the subject, write **Correct** on the line. If it does not agree, write the correct verb form.

> **EXAMPLE** Some of the invitations was mailed. *were*

1. All of the guests was eating the birthday cake. _____

2. Everyone were singing loudly. _____

3. Someone has given me a boardgame. _____

4. Most of the favors was bought at the candy store. _____

5. Both of my brothers were trying to open my gifts! _____

6. Each of the guests have played this game before. _____

7. Some of the birthday cake were eaten before the party! _____

8. Is any of the presents not opened yet? _____

9. Everything was bought at my favorite store. _____

Indefinite Pronoun Subjects

Lesson 4

More Practice

A. Making Verbs Agree with Indefinite Pronoun Subjects

In each sentence, underline the indefinite pronoun and the verb. (If a verb includes more than one word, underline only the first helping verb.) If the verb agrees with the subject, write **Correct** on the line. If it does not agree, write the correct verb form.

1. Were any of Joe's classmates not invited? _____

2. All of the invitations has his favorite cartoon character on them. _____

3. No one are going to guess the mystery guest. _____

4. Everyone wear a party hat. _____

5. A few is buying Joe one big gift. _____

6. Only some of the presents are practical, useful things. _____

7. Many of the balloons pops when they hit the ceiling here. _____

8. Most of my time at the party were spent playing two games. _____

9. Both require ten people to play them. _____

10. One of Joe's presents were barking at him! _____

B. Using Verbs with Indefinite Pronoun Subjects

Write each numbered sentence on the appropriate line, using the correct present tense form of the verb.

(1) One of my friends (be) planning a surprise birthday party for Elisa.
(2) All of her school friends (know) about the party. (3) Many (have) already bought some decorations. For example, there will be balloons and streamers.
(4) Another group (want) to bake her an extravagant cake. (5) Everybody (agree) that this will be the best surprise birthday party ever.

1. _____

2. _____

3. _____

4. _____

5. _____

Copyright © McDougal Littell/Houghton Mifflin Company.

CHAPTER 7

Indefinite Pronoun Subjects

Lesson 4

Application

A. Checking Agreement of Verbs with Indefinite Pronoun Subjects

Proofread this paragraph for errors in subject-verb agreement. Underline any verb that does not agree with the indefinite pronoun used as its subject. On a line below, write the number of each sentence with an error, and rewrite the sentence correctly.

(1) All of my birthday parties in the past few years has been exciting. **(2)** For example, one were held at the local ice skating rink. **(3)** Everyone was skating. We noticed our favorite Olympic ice skater there. **(4)** This year, both of my parents wants me to have another exciting birthday. **(5)** No one want me to be bored. **(6)** Instead, everybody expect a hot-air balloon ride this year.

_____

_____

_____

_____

_____

_____

B. Using Verbs Correctly with Indefinite Pronouns as Subjects

In each sentence beginning below, underline the word that should be used as the simple subject in a sentence. Then supply a complete predicate, using a present-tense verb of your choice, to complete the sentence. Make sure your verb agrees with its subject.

EXAMPLE All of the cake *has been eaten*.

1. Most of the cars

2. All of the gifts

3. None of the ice cream

4. Both of the twins

5. Either of the parents

6. All of the guests

7. Some of the children

8. Most of the backyard

Copyright © McDougal Littell/Houghton Mifflin Company.

CHAPTER 7

Subjects in Unusual Positions

Lesson 5

Teaching

In some sentences, unusual word order makes the subject hard to find. To be sure that the verb agrees with the subject, you first need to locate the subject.

Sentences That Begin with a Prepositional Phrase In some sentences that begin with prepositional phrases, the subject comes after the verb.

Into the river **scurried** the **otter.** (*scurried*-verb., *otter*-subject.)

Turn the sentence around, putting the subject before the verb. Then make sure that the verb agrees with the subject.

The **otter scurried** into the river.

Sentences That Begin with *Here* or *There* In most sentences that begin with *here* or *there,* the subject comes after the verb. Again, check subject-verb agreement after reordering the words of the sentence.

There **are** the **boundaries** of the farm. (*There* is not the subject; *boundaries* is.)
The **boundaries** of the farm **are** there.

Questions In many questions, the subject follows the verb or comes between parts of the verb.

Does this **river flow** south or east? (*Does flow* = verb, *river* = subject)

Change the parts around to normal word order. Then check subject-verb agreement.

This **river does flow** south or east.

A. Recognizing Verbs and Subjects in Unusual Positions

In each sentence, find and underline the verb or parts of the verb. Then find the subject and underline it twice. On the line at the right, identify whether the noun and verb are both **Singular** or **Plural.**

1. Is Susan going to the dance? _____

2. Here are my grandparents now. _____

3. There were three hats on the rack earlier. _____

4. Peacefully flows the river to the sea. _____

5. Is my brother playing on your team? _____

B. Making Verbs Agree with Subjects in Unusual Positions

Underline both the subject and the correct form of the verb in parentheses.

1. (Does, Do) snakes eat toads?

2. There (is, are) some aphids on the stem.

3. Underneath every leaf (lurks, lurk) a caterpillar.

4. (Is, Are) the ladybugs eating the aphids?

5. Into the soil (goes, go) the seeds.

6. (Does, Do) you grow corn or beans?

Copyright © McDougal Littell/Houghton Mifflin Company.

CHAPTER 7

Subjects in Unusual Positions

A. Making Verbs Agree with Subjects in Unusual Positions

In each sentence, underline the verb that agrees in number with the subject.

1. There (is, are) three nines in twenty-seven.

2. (Doesn't, Don't) Martin have any hobbies?

3. How (does, do) rain turn to snow?

4. After graduation (comes, come) the real tests.

5. To the victor (belongs, belong) the spoils.

6. (Is, Are) the job of trimming trees hard work?

7. What (does, do) that word mean?

8. Here (is, are) the way out.

9. Toward the sunset (flies, fly) the geese.

10. Once upon a time there (was, were) a poor boy and his widowed mother.

B. Correcting Subject-Verb Agreement

If the verb agrees with its subject, write **Correct** on the line. If it disagrees, write the correct form of the verb.

1. Here is my best friend's parents.   _____

2. Is he asking for Tom?   _____

3. Is raisins one of the ingredients of mincemeat?   _____

4. After the salad come the main course.   _____

5. Why do the chicken cross the road?   _____

6. Out of the darkness rises a strange figure.   _____

7. There is no more apples in the barrel.   _____

8. How do the machines in this room work?   _____

9. Don't chemistry class require special equipment?   _____

10. Here, at last, was the graduates.   _____

Copyright © McDougal Littell/Houghton Mifflin Company.

Lesson 5 Subjects in Unusual Positions   *Application*

A. Proofreading for Agreement of Verbs with Subjects in Unusual Positions

Proofread this paragraph for errors in subject-verb agreement. Draw a line through each incorrect verb. Then draw this proofreading symbol ⌃ next to the word and write the correction above the error.

There was two creepy movies on television last night. I tried to watch both of them. Have you ever seen movies like these? In the first one, there was several strange characters who visit town. With nightfall arrives more strangers. But where does they go in the daylight? There is no answers until the end of the movie. They are vampires! The second movie begins on another planet. On this planet, there is voices, but no visible bodies. Where do these voices come from? Suddenly the action moves to Earth. On the people of this world falls terrible calamities. Unfortunately, over me fell a great sleepiness. How do the story end? I never found out.

B. Using Verbs That Agree with Subjects in Unusual Positions

Each of these sentences has correct subject-verb agreement. In each, change the subject from singular to plural, or from plural to singular. Change the verb to match. Write your new sentence. Only the subject and verb should change.

EXAMPLE Down the hill slides a toboggan.
Down the hill slide several toboggans.

1. Here is your answer.

_____

2. Do the buses stop here?

_____

3. Over the hill rise the bright stars.

_____

4. Has your brother left the house yet?

_____

5. There are many reasons for the flood.

_____

Copyright © McDougal Littell/Houghton Mifflin Company.

Lesson 1

People and Cultures

Follow these rules of capitalization:

- Capitalize people's names and initials.

    Susan B. Anthony   Robert E. Lee

- Capitalize titles and the abbreviations of titles used before names or in direct address. Capitalize the abbreviations of some titles when they follow a name.

    Captain Pierce   Dr. David Arnold   Hello, Ambassador.   Sara Mines, Ph.D.

- Capitalize titles of heads of state, royalty, or nobility only when they are used with a person's name or in place of a person's name. Do not capitalize titles when they are used without a proper name.

    Sir Laurence Olivier   The Queen of England rode in the procession.

    The king sat on the throne.

- Capitalize the titles indicating family relationships only when the titles are used as names or parts of names. Do not capitalize a family name when it follows the person's name or is used without a proper name.

    Aunt Grace   Uncle Jim   My brother plays the bass guitar.

- Always capitalize the pronoun I.

- Capitalize the names of religions, sacred days, sacred writings, and deities. Do not capitalize the words *god* or *goddess* when they refer to figures of ancient mythology.

    Judaism   Christmas   Bible   Allah

- Capitalize the names of nationalities, languages, races, and some ethnic groups, and the adjectives formed from these names.

    Mexican   Native American   Caucasian

Capitalizing Names of People and Cultures

Underline the words that should be capitalized in each of the following sentences.

1. We learned that queen victoria reigned in England for 63 years.
2. On vacation, we bought some lovely navajo blankets.
3. My sister is dr. april c. weaver, m.d.
4. My uncle charles is a colonel in the U.S. Army.
5. My grandfather and i love swedish meatballs.
6. The speaker at our assembly was sergeant arlene m. hayes.
7. We had a delicious chinese dinner at uncle wen's house.
8. My neighbors celebrated hanukkah in December.
9. The first book of the bible is named genesis.
10. The speech was written by justice thurgood marshall of the Supreme Court.

Copyright © McDougal Littell/Houghton Mifflin Company.

CHAPTER 8

People and Cultures

Lesson 1

More Practice

A. Capitalizing Names

Underline the letters that should be capitalalized in each of the following sentences. If the sentence is already correct, write **Correct.**

1. Why did auntie em scold dorothy and her dog named toto? _____

2. My younger brother likes to read books by dr. seuss and maurice sendak. _____

3. The forget-me-not, a flower, was the emblem of king henry IV of England. _____

4. The muslims follow the teachings of mohammed. _____

5. The italian artist michelangelo painted scenes from the bible. _____

6. My mother and aunt leslie go to the same doctor, marsha lopez, m.d. _____

7. My uncle jesse is an expert on african art. _____

8. In 1881, president james a. garfield was assassinated. _____

9. My mother and i met reverend jefferson last easter. _____

10. The ancient egyptians believed their god anubis had the head of a jackal. _____

B. Capitalizing Correctly

Underline each word that should be capitalized in the following paragraph.

(1) After World War II, many european cities lay in ruins. **(2)** An american, secretary of state george c. marshall, suggested a plan to help european countries. **(3)** This plan came to be known as the Marshall Plan in honor of george c. marshall. **(4)** Marshall was an american soldier and statesman. **(5)** During World War I, captain marshall had served as an aide to general john j. pershing. **(6)** During World War II, marshall made the United States Army a great fighting force. **(7)** After the war, president harry s. truman appointed marshall secretary of state. **(8)** Marshall's role in european recovery won him a Nobel Peace Prize.

Copyright © McDougal Littell/Houghton Mifflin Company.

CHAPTER 8

People and Cultures

Lesson 1

Application

A. Proofreading

Proofread the following first draft of a report. Look especially for errors in capitalization. Draw three lines under each letter that should be capitalized.

EXAMPLE Sam <u>h</u>ouston was an <u>a</u>merican hero.

As a boy on a Tennessee farm, sam houston did not like being bossed around by his older brothers. So, at the age of 16, sam ran away and lived with the cherokees. Sam was so happy with the cherokees that chief oolooteka adopted him. Three years later, however, sam decided to become a soldier. After that, he became congressman houston, then governor houston of Tennessee. But sam grew restless, and soon he took off for Texas. At that time Texas was still under mexican rule. The american settlers were not getting along with the mexican government. Sam raised and led an army against the mexicans. He won a big victory over general santa anna. Sam became president houston of the Republic of Texas. When Texas became a state, sam became senator houston and, finally, governor houston. Sam always made sure that he wasn't going to be bossed around.

B. Writing with Capital Letters

You have probably heard many news broadcasts in your life. Write a fictional newscast for one day. Give the news about at least five different people. Use at least three of these names and titles in your news stories. Be sure to capitalize correctly.

| senator | Jr. | M.D. | queen | uncle |
| American | reverend | Mrs. | I | Mexican |

_____

_____

_____

_____

_____

_____

_____

Copyright © McDougal Littell/Houghton Mifflin Company.

CHAPTER 8

Lesson 2

First Words and Titles

Teaching

Capitalize these words:

- the first word of every sentence
- the first word of every line of traditional poetry
- the first word of a direct quotation if it is a complete sentence (Do not capitalize the first word of the second part of a divided quotation unless it starts a new sentence.)

> "Our class is reading *To Kill a Mockingbird,*" said Claire.
> "I think," she said, "that the book tells a fascinating story."

- the first word of each item in an outline and letters that introduce major subsections

    I. Proper nutrition
      A. Basic food groups
        1. Breads and grains
        2. Meat, fish, and poultry

- the first word in the greeting of a letter and the first word in the closing
- the first word, the last word, and all other important words in titles (Don't capitalize articles, conjunctions, or prepositions of fewer than five letters.)

Capitalizing First Words and Titles

Underline the words that should be capitalized in each of the following items.

1. "one of my favorite authors," Nathan said, "is William Faulkner."
2. Carlos asked, "what has he written, Nathan?"
3. another student replied, "he wrote both short stories and novels."
4. "yes, his most famous short story is 'the bear.'"
5. I. William Faulkner

    a. childhood

    b. writing career

      1. early career

      2. creation of Yoknapatawpha County novels

6. nearly all of his books take place in the fictional Yoknapatawpha County.
7. dear Mrs. Powell,

    Since you are the head librarian at our school library, I am asking you to purchase a copy of *the sound and the fury* by William Faulkner.

    sincerely,

    Rusty

8. Al asked, "is it true that some of Faulkner's characters are in several of his books?"
9. did you know that Faulkner was famous for writing extremely long sentences?

Copyright © McDougal Littell/Houghton Mifflin Company.

First Words and Titles

More Practice

A. Capitalizing First Words and Titles

In the following sentences underline the words that should be capitalized but are not. If the sentence contains no capitalization errors, write **Correct** on the line.

1. Arthur Miller wrote the award-winning play *death of a salesman*.

2. when I was young, my favorite book was *anne of green gables*.

3. dear Uncle Eric,

   Thank you for recommending to me *i, robot* by Isaac Asimov. you know I always enjoy a good science fiction book.

                                 sincerely,

                                 Pam

4. brown and furry

caterpillar in a hurry

take your walk

to the shady leaf or stalk.

                    Christina Georgina Rossetti, "The Caterpillar"

5. "My favorite books," said Angelo, "are mysteries, especially Sherlock Holmes stories."

6. some poems are written about real people, such as "paul revere's ride."

7. Even though Paul Revere was a real person, that poem is not entirely factual.

8. "it seems," Shelby said, "that *moby dick* must be the longest book ever written."

B. Capitalizing First Words in Outlines

Underline each letter that should be capitalized in the following outline.

Native Americans of the Northeast

  I. cultural groups

 II. important foods

    a. lake nations

      1. wild rice

      2. fish and shellfish

    b. woodland nations

      1. corn, squash, and beans

      2. deer and other game

Copyright © McDougal Littell/Houghton Mifflin Company.

First Words and Titles   *Application*

A. Writing a Letter

Imagine that you have a pen pal in a different school. Write a letter to that pen pal.
Name and describe at least three good books, short stories, or poems you have
read, either by yourself or in class. Be sure to capitalize your letter correctly.

_____

_____

_____

_____

_____

_____

B. Writing an Outline Using Capital Letters Correctly

Read the following brief report. Then write a short outline for it on the lines below.
Be sure to capitalize correctly.

Louisa May Alcott was an author who grew up in Massachusetts. Because
her father, Bronson Alcott, was a teacher and a great thinker, she received an
unusually fine education. She was tutored by the writers Ralph Waldo
Emerson and Henry David Thoreau. During the Civil War she served as a
nurse.

To supply her poor family with at least some money, Ms. Alcott wrote
exciting stories called *thrillers* for popular magazines. But her most enduring
contribution was her family novels. Her most famous work is *Little Women*,
an autobiographical novel of her childhood and family life in New England.

The Life of Louisa May Alcott

  I. Early life

_____

_____

  II. Later life

_____

_____

Copyright © McDougal Littell/Houghton Mifflin Company.

Lesson 3

Places and Transportation

Teaching

Follow these rules of capitalization:

- In geographical names, capitalize each word except articles and prepositions. Geographical names include the names of continents *(Africa)*, bodies of water *(Red Sea)*, islands *(Bahamas)*, mountains *(Andes Mountains)*, other landforms *(Gobi Desert)*, world regions *(Middle East)*, nations *(Ethiopia)*, states *(Oregon)*, cities *(Philadelphia)*, and streets *(Elm Street)*.

- Capitalize the names of planets and other specific objects in the universe.

    Saturn   Big Dipper

- Capitalize the words north, south, east, and west when they name particular regions of the country or world, or when they are parts of proper names. Do not capitalize words that indicate general directions or locations.

    North America   We flew north to Alaska.

- Capitalize the names of specific buildings, bridges, monuments, and other landmarks.

    Jewel Cave   Mackinac Bridge

- Capitalize the names of specific airplanes, trains, ships, cars, and spacecraft.

    Santa Maria   *Orient Express*

Capitalizing Names and Places

Underline the words that should be capitalized in each of the following sentences. If the item is capitalized correctly, write **Correct** on the line.

1. I have spent nearly my entire life in new england. _____

2. I would love to travel to europe someday. _____

3. It would be so exciting to go to russia. _____

4. I want to see moscow, especially the kremlin, which was the seat of government for the former soviet union. _____

5. The kremlin is located on one side of historic red square. _____

6. Moscow is west of the Ural Mountains. _____

7. Its major streets, such as outer ring road, circle the kremlin. _____

8. I would travel around Moscow on their subway system, called Metro. _____

9. I also love ballet and would love to see a production at the bolshoi theatre. _____

Copyright © McDougal Littell/Houghton Mifflin Company.

CHAPTER 8

Places and Transportation

Lesson 3

More Practice

A. Capitalizing Names and Places

Underline the words that should be capitalized in each of the following sentences.
If the item is capitalized correctly, write **Correct** on the line.

1. This summer, my family took a trip to philadelphia, pennsylvania. _____

2. It is in the southeast corner of the state where the delaware river and
   schuylkill river meet. _____

3. My favorite place there was the franklin institute science museum. _____

4. It is the oldest museum of applied sciences in the united states. _____

5. We saw a show at the Fels Planetarium about different stars and planets. _____

6. The speaker pointed out planets we can see, such as venus, mars,
   and jupiter. _____

7. I also learned about constellations, such as the big dipper and orion. _____

8. The show taught us that *apollo 11* was the first manned spacecraft to
   land on the moon. _____

9. It was also exciting to see Philadelphia's independence hall. _____

10. We saw the famous City Hall where broad street and market
    street intersect. _____

11. Philadelphia was the first city in north America to be based on a
    rectangular grid pattern. _____

B. Capitalizing Names of Places in a Paragraph

Underline the words that should be capitalized in the following paragraph.

lima is the capital and biggest city in peru, a country in south america. The
city is located on the pacific ocean. lima's population is 6.4 million, which is
close to one-third of the total population of peru. The andes mountains are to
the east of the city. Most of Lima's landmarks are in the old colonial part of
town, south of the rímac river. Many of the sites are centered around a busy
plaza. Famous sites include a cathedral and the government palace, home of
peru's president. A busy street connects the Plaza de Armas to the plaza san
martín. lima is a major city in south america, along with cities such as são
paulo and buenos aries.

Copyright © McDougal Littell/Houghton Mifflin Company.

Lesson 3

Places and Transportation   *Application*

A. Proofreading

Proofread this paragraph about a guided tour of Manila. Underline every word that
needs to be capitalized.

      manila is a huge, historic city at the center of a metropolitan area of 246
square miles on luzon island. Tagalog is the local language, but English is used
in businesses and schools. The pasig river divides the original city on the
southern bank from the modern part, which is on the northern bank. Most of
the tourist sites are in the old area along roxas boulevard, which runs parallel
to manila bay. In 1571, spain conquered manila and ruled it for the next 350
years. During the Spanish-American War at the end of the 19th century,
Manila was a target for American forces. In 1898 Commodore George Dewey
attacked Manila with his cruisers, *olympia, baltimore, boston,* and *raleigh.* He
easily destroyed the Spanish fleet, and manila became the center of the U.S.
administration in southeast asia. Today, Manila is the capital of the philippines.

B. Using Capital Letters in Writing

Choose one real place that you would like to visit someday. It could be near the
ocean or in the mountains. It could be a big city or a remote national park. In a
paragraph on the lines below, name the place and tell where it is and what natural
features (rivers, lakes, mountains) it is near.

_____

_____

_____

_____

_____

_____

_____

_____

_____

_____

Copyright © McDougal Littell/Houghton Mifflin Company.

CHAPTER 8

Lesson 4 · Organizations and Other Subjects · *Teaching*

Use capital letters for the following:

- all important words in names of organizations, institutions, stores, and companies

  National Organization of Women   **Boston University**   **Davis Bicycle Shop**

- names of historical events, periods, and documents

  French Revolution   **Ice Age**   **Treaty of Versailles**

- the abbreviations B.C., A.D., A.M., and P.M.

  12:12 P.M.   **250** A.D.

- names of months, days, and holidays but not the names of seasons, except when used as part of a festival or celebration

  Thursday   **Flag Day**   **Annual Fall Homecoming**

- names of special events and awards

  San Marino Rodeo   **Pulitzer Prize**

- brand names of products but not a common noun that follows a brand name

  Velvet Smooth hand lotion   **Ever Bright** toothpaste

Identifying Correct Capitalization

Underline the words or letters that should be capitalized in each of the following sentences.

1. On april 14, 1865, President Abraham Lincoln was shot.
2. He had been watching a play at ford theater in Washington, D.C.
3. Lincoln was president during an important part of our nation's history, the civil war.
4. The American Civil War began in a.d. june 1861.
5. One of President Lincoln's major accomplishments was writing the emancipation proclamation.
6. During his administration, an act was signed forming two railroad companies, the union pacific and the central pacific.
7. On inauguration day in 1861, Lincoln rejected the right of a state to secede from the Union.
8. Lincoln had served in the military during the black hawk war in 1830.
9. William Lloyd Garrison began the american anti-slavery society.
10. The Land-Grant Acts started many schools, including cornell university.

Copyright © McDougal Littell/Houghton Mifflin Company.

CHAPTER 8

Lesson 4 · Organizations and Other Subjects

More Practice

A. Capitalizing Names of Organizations and Other Subjects

Underline each word that should be capitalized in the following sentences.

1. The school bus picks us up at 7 a.m.
2. Each year, the nobel peace prize is awarded to someone who has furthered the cause of peace.
3. My grandmother makes her potato salad with jordan's mayonnaise.
4. The american civil liberties union defends Americans' rights.
5. The Midvale carpenters union always walks in the city parade on labor day.
6. Many of the houses in my neighborhood were built in the victorian style.
7. Sheila is an avid bird watcher and belongs to the national audubon society.
8. The magna carta was signed by King John in England in 1215.
9. My sister attends the university of nebraska.
10. Mr. Patrick Daniels began the p.d. shoe company in 1855.

B. Capitalizing Correctly

Rewrite every sentence that contains a capitalization error. If a sentence is capitalized correctly, write **Correct** on the line.

1. Last fall the soccer team awarded James the most valuable player award.

_____

2. My grandfather began his own plumbing company, cincotta and sons.

_____

3. melfield middle school will have its melfield winter concert on december 15.

_____

4. My family goes skiing every year in february on presidents' day.

_____

5. Don't you agree that Twisty Dough pretzels are the best pretzels you can buy?

_____

6. At 7 a.m. electronics warehouse will open its doors for the biggest sale ever.

_____

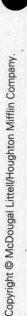

Copyright © McDougal Littell/Houghton Mifflin Company.

Organizations and Other Subjects

Lesson 4

Application

A. Proofreading for Capitalization Errors

Read the following speech given at the awards ceremony at a middle school. Draw three lines under any letters that should be capitalized but are not.

EXAMPLE As principal, I welcome you to the special award ceremony.

Vienna middle school is proud to have sent the team that won first prize at the annual autumn history bee. To prepare for the event, these students studied every day after school from 3:00 p.m. to 6:00 p.m. Their hard work and dedication finally paid off when they traveled to george washington university this past october on columbus day. The competition's questions were written by the american history bee association. The topics ranged from the american revolution and the great depression to the cold war. Among the many facts our students knew were the following: the number of amendments in the bill of rights and the writer of the declaration of independence. For their outstanding performances, I hereby award them with the Vienna middle school scholar award.

B. Using Capitalization in Writing

First, choose two categories to combine from those listed below. Then write a sentence that uses a proper noun from each category. Be sure that you have capitalized all the proper nouns correctly.

organizations	institutions	stores	companies	historical events
historical periods	documents	days	months	holidays
events		awards	brand names	time abbreviations

EXAMPLE I am combining *stores and institutions.*
The Village Market is near the Brookdale Hospital.

1. I am combining _____ and _____.

Sentence: _____

2. I am combining _____ and _____.

Sentence: _____

3. I am combining _____ and _____.

Sentence: _____

Copyright © McDougal Littell/Houghton Mifflin Company.

Lesson 1 — Periods and Other End Marks

Teaching

The three end marks are the period, question mark, and exclamation point.

Periods Use a period at the end of a **declarative sentence,** which makes a statement.

> Jupiter is the fifth planet from the sun.

Use a period at the end of almost every **imperative sentence.** An imperative sentence gives a command. If a command is said with emotion, it ends in an exclamation point.

> Put that book away. Put it away!

Use a period at the end of an **indirect question.** An indirect question reports what a person asked without using the person's exact words.

> Thomas asked if we had read the map correctly.

Use a period after an **abbreviation** or an **initial,** as in this example: Dr. Mary J. Smith

Use a period after each number and letter in an **outline** or **list.**

Question marks Use a question mark to end an **interrogative sentence,** or question.

> Where exactly is Napoleon, Ohio?

Exclamation points Use an exclamation point to end an **exclamatory sentence,** that is, a sentence that expresses strong feeling. Use an exclamation point after an **interjection.**

> Wow! What a beautiful view!

Using Periods and Other End Marks

Add punctuation as necessary in the following items.

1. Does your friend Brandon C Mitchell live in New York City
2. New York City has more people than many countries have
3. Incredible Just imagine ten million people on the city streets at the same time
4. How difficult it must be to get to school or work
5. The bus arrives at 7:23 AM
6. How often does the C train run
7. Write an essay about the various forms of transportation in New York City
8. I The 19th century
   A Horse-drawn buggies
   B Horse-drawn buses
   II The 20th century
   A Motorized vehicles
   B The subway
9. The passenger asked whether the bus stopped at the zoo
10. Why are these streets so narrow

Copyright © McDougal Littell/Houghton Mifflin Company.

Lesson 1 **Periods and Other End Marks** *More Practice*

A. Using Periods and Other End Marks

Add punctuation marks where necessary in the following items.

1. Mr Smith asked the conductor if the train stopped in Smithtown
2. Does this train stop in Smithtown
3. Do you know the way to Green Springs Middle School
4. Dr C Everett Koop was US surgeon general
5. The train to Chicago departed at 8:27 AM
6. Look out for that car
7. Can you read German
8. We won We won Can you believe it
9. What cities are located along Route 66
10. Tell me the names of those cities again
11. I   Important American rivers
    A Mississippi River
    B Tennessee River
    C Missouri River
    D Rio Grande River
12. Attention Listen to these instructions

B. Using Periods and Other End Marks in Writing

Add the correct end mark at the end of each sentence in the following paragraph.

In a city with the population of New York City, transportation is a top

priority__ So many vehicles are needed each day__ New York meets this need

by providing many kinds of transportation__ The city's three subway systems

are used day and night__ If you want to travel in style, how can you get to

your destination __ Try hailing a cab__ New York's many bridges transport cars

and buses from borough to borough__ What is a good tip to remember if you

go to New York City__ Do a little research to find out the best way to get

where you want to go__

Copyright © McDougal Littell/Houghton Mifflin Company.

CHAPTER 9

Lesson 1

Periods and Other End Marks   *Application*

A. Using Periods and Other End Marks in Writing

Add periods, question marks, and exclamation points where necessary in the following paragraph. To add a period, insert this symbol ⊙. To add a question mark or an exclamation point, use a caret ⌃ and write the correct punctuation mark above it.

Traveling by airplane may be fast, but traveling by train is interesting, educational, and fun If you don't have the extra time, you could take a plane But what would you see on the plane You might see the sky, the clouds, or maybe a movie On the train, you can sit back, look out the window, and see real people, real places, cities, towns, mountains, plains, and rivers What interesting sights you will pass It's true that on the plane you often are served food Yet how many people really like airline food The food can be much better on the train because you bring your own So, if you're looking for a good way to get from here to there, why always look to the skies Your best bet might be as close as the nearest railroad station

B. Using Periods in an Outline

Write an outline for a composition about differences between fifth grade and sixth grade. Give the outline a title, and, using the outline form given below, compare two topics (such as teachers, homework, sports, school responsibilities) for each year. Be sure to punctuate the outline correctly.

Title: _____

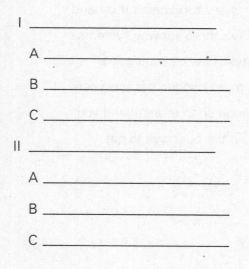

I _____

   A _____

   B _____

   C _____

II _____

   A _____

   B _____

   C _____

Copyright © McDougal Littell/Houghton Mifflin Company.

Lesson 2 Commas in Sentences   *Teaching*

In a series of three or more items, use a comma after every item except the last one.

> **Pocahontas, her husband, and their son sailed to England in 1616.**

Use commas between two or more adjectives of equal rank that modify the same noun. The adjectives are of equal rank if you can substitute the word *and* for the comma.

> **Pocahontas was a brave, powerful woman.**

Use commas after an introductory word or phrase.

> **As an adult, Pocahontas converted to Christianity.**

Use commas to set off one or more words that interrupt the flow of thought in a sentence.

> **The legend about her saving the life of John Smith, by the way, is probably false.**

Use commas to set off nouns of direct address.

> **During her life, my friend, she met the King and Queen of England.**

Use commas to set off nonessential appositives. Appositives are nonessential if the meaning of the sentence is clear without them.

> **Her marriage to John Rolfe, a colonist, led to eight years of peace.**

Use a comma whenever the reader might otherwise be confused.

> **Before her return home, smallpox ended her life.**

Using Commas Correctly

Insert commas where necessary in the following sentences.

1. The Comanche leader Chief Quanah wanted to preserve the Comanche lifestyle.
2. Spanish explorers also known as conquistadors searched for the legendary city of gold.
3. After the death of his father and brother Metacomet became chief of the Wampanoags.
4. Philip by the way was the name the English settlers gave to Metacomet.
5. Philip his people and a group of other Native Americans led an uprising called King Philip's War.
6. Did you know Dad that the colonists broke all the treaties signed by Philip and his father?
7. Chief Pontiac led a long difficult siege against Detroit in 1763.
8. Cochise chief of the Chiricahua Apache eventually agreed to remain on a reservation.

Copyright © McDougal Littell/Houghton Mifflin Company.

Commas in Sentences

Lesson 2

More Practice

A. Using Commas

Insert commas where necessary in the following sentences.

1. Chief Joseph was a strong intelligent chief of the Nez Perce in the western United States.

2. Following in his father's footsteps Chief Joseph refused to keep his people on a reservation.

3. Kathy violence broke out when the United States tried to enforce a treaty.

4. After agreeing to leave the Oregon Territory Joseph then decided to take his people to Canada.

5. Thirty miles from the border troops stopped the Nez Perce after a five-day battle.

6. Unfortunately many Nez Perce died of illnesses when they were sent to Oklahoma.

7. Sitting Bull chief of the Sioux was another chief who ran into trouble with U.S. authorities.

8. Sitting Bull Crazy Horse and others defeated General Custer's men at the Battle of the Little Bighorn.

9. After returning to the United States from Canada Sitting Bull was put in prison for two years.

10. Surprisingly Sitting Bull was allowed to leave the reservation to tour with Buffalo Bill's Wild West Show.

B. Using Commas in Writing

Rewrite the following paragraph, using commas where they are needed.

Geronimo another chief of the Chiricahua Apache was born in what is now Arizona. Mexicans killed his wife children and mother in 1858. He settled down nevertheless on a reservation. According to my history book the American government tried to move his tribe to New Mexico. Geronimo I can understand why you fought the move and tried to defend your lands. An American general George Crook captured Geronimo. Escaping from federal troops several times Geronimo surrendered for the last time in 1886. Sadly for him his people were separated and sent to Florida Alabama and Oklahoma.

_____

_____

_____

_____

_____

_____

CHAPTER 9

Copyright © McDougal Littell/Houghton Mifflin Company.

Lesson 2 Commas in Sentences   *Application*

A. Writing with Complete Subjects and Complete Predicates

Add commas there they are needed in the following paragraph. Use the proofreading symbol ^, .

    Black Hawk also knows as Ma-ka-tae-mish-kia-kiak was chief of his people in what is now Illinois and Wisconsin. At first he agreed to sell his traditional lands east of the Mississippi River to the United States. He argued later that the whites had unfairly forced the Native Americans to agree to the sale. During the War of 1812 Black Hawk fought alongside the British. Black Hawk the Sac people and the Fox people were forced west in 1823. They suffered from hunger in their new less-fertile lands. Desperate to survive they tried to return to their old lands to grow more food. White settlers shot Black Hawk's aide. Black Hawk not surprisingly began what is now known as the Black Hawk War. After surrendering in August 1832 he and his people were forced to settle on a reservation in Iowa.

B. Using Commas in Writing

Rewrite the sentences by following the directions in parentheses.

1. Native Americans grew many vegetables. (Add a series of items.)

_____

2. The Apaches fought in the battle. (Add two adjectives of equal rank that modify the same noun.)

_____

3. Several Native American groups were forced out of Ohio. (Add an introductory phrase.)

_____

_____

4. Native Americans were often treated unfairly in their homeland. (Add an appositive.)

_____

_____

Copyright © McDougal Littell/Houghton Mifflin Company.

CHAPTER 9

Lesson 3

Commas: Dates, Addresses, and Letters   *Teaching*

Commas in dates Use a comma between the day of the month and the year. If the sentence continues, use a comma after the year, also.

>On November 11, 1918, the armistice was signed.

Commas in addresses Use a comma between the name of a city or town and the name of the state or country. If the sentence continues, use a comma after the name of the state or country.

>The zoo in Buffalo, New York, is in Delaware Park.

Commas in letters Use a comma after the greeting of an informal letter and after the closing of an informal or business letter.

>Dear Dad,   Your daughter,

A. Using Commas Correctly in Dates and Addresses

Insert commas where necessary in the following sentences.

1. General Douglas MacArthur was born on January 26 1880 in Little Rock Arkansas.

2. My aunt wrote a letter to me on July 12 1992 from Ann Arbor Michigan but hasn't written since.

3. I remember the city of Ypsilanti Michigan well.

4. We promised we would get together again on July 1 2020 at the town park.

5. Many older people remember where they were on November 22 1963 when President John Kennedy was shot in Dallas Texas.

6. The stock market crash on October 29 1929 was known as "Black Tuesday."

B. Using Commas Correctly in Dates, Addresses, and Letters

Insert commas where necessary in the following letter.

March 9 2002

Dear Uncle Mike

Thanks for taking us to the Milwaukee Zoo. We got back on March 6 2002 from our vacation. The zoo visit was all we could talk about during the rest of the trip. Before we came home, we stopped off in Columbus Ohio to see Mom's old college roommate. Hope you'll come to see us in Buffalo New York one of these days.

Love

Tess

Copyright © McDougal Littell/Houghton Mifflin Company.

Commas: Dates, Addresses, and Letters

Lesson 3

More Practice

A. Using Commas Correctly in Dates and Addresses

Insert commas where necessary in the following sentences.

1. My grandfather told us that on January 3 1950 two feet of snow fell on his town.

2. The first Independence Day was July 4 1776.

3. Chris was born in Chicago Illinois but moved to Madison Wisconsin.

4. Did the millennium begin on January 1 2000 or January 1 2001?

5. I've never been to Rome Italy, but I have been to Rome New York.

6. I don't know whether this program comes from Portland Oregon or Portland Maine.

7. We will meet again in Tucson Arizona on June 6 2005.

8. The return address was 217 Sherman St., Syracuse NY.

B. Writing with Commas

Write these parts in the correct order on the lines below. Use commas where they are needed.

600 Sutton Lane	Your friend	I can hardly wait to see you in Cape Cod Massachusetts next week. We are driving through Newport Rhode Island on our way. I hope the weather on the ocean is clear and sunny, but we will have a great time no matter what the weather is.
Arnetta	Dear Tess	
Skokie IL 60076	July 15 2001	

_____

_____

_____

_____

_____

_____

_____

_____

_____

_____

_____

Copyright © McDougal Littell/Houghton Mifflin Company.

Lesson 3

Commas: Dates, Addresses, and Letters   *Application*

A. Proofreading a Letter

Proofread the following letter for punctuation errors. Insert commas where necessary.

534 Wesley Drive
Cleveland OH 44108
March 12 2001

Dear Luisa

   I though you might like to hear about my trip to Buffalo. My cousins Teddy and Jimmy are really into sports! On March 6 2001 we went to this great zoo in West County New York. It's old but huge, and the animals seem to like it a lot. Teddy said the zoo was build during the Depression. I think it must have been one of the projects like the ones your dad worked on. Did he ever work in Buffalo New York?

   I hope you're coming home from Guadeloupe Mexico in time for my birthday party next month.

See you later
Carmine

B. Writing with Commas

Write a letter from a vacation spot somewhere in the world. Address your letter to a relative or a good friend. In your letter, tell about two things you have seen or done on the vacation so far. Use the form of an informal letter, and use commas correctly. Include a return address (you can make up a ZIP code if you don't know it) and a greeting before the body of the letter, and a closing and your signature after the body of the letter.

_____

_____

_____

_____

_____

_____

_____

_____

_____

_____

_____

_____

Copyright © McDougal Littell/Houghton Mifflin Company.

Punctuating Quotations   *Teaching*

Lesson 4

A **direct quotation** is a speaker's exact words. Use quotation marks at the beginning and at the end of a direct quotation.

>   "These games are a challenge," Joe declared.

Use commas to set off the explanatory words used with a direct quotation, at the beginning, middle, or end of the quotation.

>   Jose declared, "These games are a challenge."

>   "These games," Joe declared, "are a challenge."

If the quotation itself is a question or exclamation, the question mark or exclamation point falls inside the end quotation marks. Commas and periods always go inside the end quotation marks.

>   "Oh no!" Nina cried. "Where's my notebook?"

If the quotation is part of a question or an exclamation, the question mark or exclamation point falls outside the end quotation marks.

>   Did Francesca say, "Buy me a gold sweater"?

A **divided quotation** is a direct quotation that is divided into two parts by explanatory words. Both parts are enclosed in quotation marks. The first word in the second part is not capitalized unless it begins a sentence. Review the above examples to see how to punctuate and capitalize a divided quotation.

A **dialogue** is a conversation between two or more speakers. In writing a dialogue, indicate a change in speaker by using a new paragraph and new set of quotation marks.

>   "Sunita," Anne asked, "are these the pants you bought last week?"
>   "Yes, they were such a bargain," Sunita answered.

An **indirect quotation** is a restatement, in somewhat different words, of what someone said. Do not use quotation marks to set off an indirect quotation.

>   The manager announced that the store is closing.

Using Quotation Marks

Add quotation marks and commas where necessary in each of these sentences.

1. Did the saleswoman say We're having a sale on sport watches?

2. Wait! Patrick yelled. My aunt said the sale doesn't start until tomorrow.

3. My mother would like this sweater said Chad.

4. Margaret asked Which perfume smells nicer?
Well Nina replied I like the first bottle best.

5. The silver bracelet will make a nice gift said Andre.

6. The cashier said that the store was really busy this morning.

7. My shopping cart Judy announced is packed!

8. The cashier asked Who's next in line?

Copyright © McDougal Littell/Houghton Mifflin Company.

CHAPTER 9

Lesson 4

Punctuating Quotations

More Practice

A. Writing Sentences with Quotation Marks

Add quotation marks and commas where necessary in each sentence. If the sentence is correct as is, circle the number of the sentence.

1. Darn! Clara said. I paid $10 more for these pants just yesterday.
2. This radio the salesperson announced has excellent sound quality.
3. Gretchen told me last week that this store has a great selection.
4. Didn't Ted say Meet me in the shoe department at noon?
5. Faisal asked How do you like this hat?
   I think it looks outstanding on you Simone replied.
6. The sale items explained the manager are all sold out.
7. Didn't my brother say asked Erika that he wanted a blue hat for his birthday?
8. These towels exclaimed Angela are so soft!
9. Isn't this dress asked Viv amazingly beautiful?
10. Mrs. Rogers said Finding the right pair of shoes can be a trying experience.

B. Using Quotation Marks

Copy this dialogue below, add quotation marks where necessary.

I'd like to get my mother something nice for her birthday, Ross said.

Does she like flowers? asked Jeremy. Flowers are a good gift.

But, Ross answered, I got her flowers last year.

Jeremy agreed that Ross should think of something else.

I know! Jeremy exclaimed. You can get her a cat.

Ross yelled, Perfect! That's a great idea!

_____

_____

_____

_____

_____

_____

_____

_____

_____

Copyright © McDougal Littell/Houghton Mifflin Company.

Copyright © McDougal Littell/Houghton Mifflin Company.

Lesson 4 Punctuating Quotations   *Application*

A. Correcting Misuse of Quotation Marks

Rewrite the following sentences, adding or replacing quotation marks, commas, and end marks correctly.

1. Great!" Ashok cried. "I've been looking all day for the perfect pair of jeans.

_____

_____

2. Which jacket asked Mr. Cox, will keep me the warmest this winter.

_____

3. You should buy it now because you might not have another chance said Paul.

_____

_____

4. Kayla said I would really like to buy this book on Thomas Jefferson for my father.

_____

_____

5. Did your brother say Please get a backpack from the mall.

_____

B. Writing with Quotation Marks

Write a short dialogue that you might overhear in a clothing store. Make sure that you indicate clearly who is speaking. Use quotation marks and other punctuation marks correctly.

_____

_____

_____

_____

_____

_____

_____

_____

_____

Semicolons and Colons

Lesson 5

CHAPTER 9

Teaching

Semicolons in Compound Sentences Use a semicolon to join the parts of a compound sentence if you don't use a coordinating conjunction.

> The night was clear; the stars were bright.

Semicolons with Items in a Series When there are commas within parts of a series, use a semicolon to separate the parts.

> John was from Ames, Iowa; Helen was from Butler, Pennsylvania; and Linda was from Rockford, Illinois.

Colons Use a colon in the following ways: after the formal greeting in a business letter, between hours and minutes in expressions of time, and to introduce a list of items. When using the colon to introduce a list, use it only after nouns or pronouns.

> Dear Judge Hogan:

> The Town Board meeting starts at 7:30 P.M. The board will discuss three topics: sewers, schools, and taxes.

Using Semicolons and Colons

Add semicolons and colons where they are needed in the following sentences.

1. Yellow jackets are a kind of wasp their smooth, brown bodies are marked with yellow stripes.

2. That story is science fiction it's based on weird but believable scientific ideas.

3. The pickup truck roared down the dirt road huge clouds of dust trailed behind it.

4. We will need several items for the first-aid kit gauze, a small scissors, first-aid cream, tape, and bandages.

5. The bridal party included the bride's sister, Raquel her best friend, Theresa and the groom's sister, Janet.

6. The Venus flytrap is an unusual plant it eats insects.

7. H. G. Wells wrote many kinds of literature science fiction, history, and novels.

8. Here's the shopping list bread, milk, tuna, apples, and artichoke hearts.

9. The movie started at 930 by 700 the ticket line stretched around the corner.

10. Bram Stoker was Irish the Dracula myth is Slavic.

11. We will read stories by the following writers Edgar Allan Poe, Nathaniel Hawthorne, and Henry James.

12. In spring, set the clock ahead 700 becomes 800.

13. Jules Verne is considered the father of science fiction he wrote *Twenty Thousand Leagues Under the Sea.*

14. A tiny car stops in the middle of the circus ring a crowd of clowns pop out of the car.

Copyright © McDougal Littell/Houghton Mifflin Company.

Lesson 5

Semicolons and Colons

More Practice

A. Using the Semicolon and the Colon

Add semicolons and colons where they are needed in the numbered sentences.

(1) Jules Verne may not be the father of science fiction an earlier writer may actually have invented science fiction. **(2)** Edmond Rostand wrote a famous play about this person his name is Cyrano de Bergerac.

(3) Verne and Rostand both wrote in the last half of the 19th century the real Cyrano lived in the 17th century. **(4)** The real-life Cyrano and the Cyrano in the play had many memorable qualities a lively imagination, a way with words, and a long nose. **(5)** In the play, Cyrano assumes a disguise, he pretends he's an alien from the moon who has fallen to Earth. The real Cyrano had been a soldier in the French army and only later became a writer. **(6)** Cyrano's topics were typical science fiction ideas rocket ships, travel to other planets, and space exploration. It took 300 years for science and technology to catch up to his imagination.

B. Using the Semicolon and the Colon in Writing

On the line at the right, write the word(s) from the sentence that should be followed by a semicolon or colon. Write the correct punctuation mark following each word. If the sentence is punctuated correctly, write **Correct.**

1. That book was a bestseller it sold out in a week. _____

2. Readers seemed to like three things about the book the complicated plot, the funny characters, and the strange setting. _____

3. Marchers in the parade included the Blazers, a band from Nebraska; the Lawnmower Brigade, a group from Indiana and the Gators, a cheerleading squad from Florida. _____

4. Hugo was shot from a cannon he sailed across the circus tent. _____

5. I thanked my piano teacher, Mrs. Johnson; the lady who had hosted the recital, Mrs. Torgersen; and my parents, Mr. and Mrs. Donaldson. _____

6. Bryan's collection includes stamps from these countries Zimbabwe, Ethiopia, and Kenya. _____

7. The movie begins at 710 P.M. and ends at 920 P.M. _____

8. Don't forget these items at the grocery store: milk, bread, and lettuce. _____

Copyright © McDougal Littell/Houghton Mifflin Company.

CHAPTER 9

CHAPTER 9

Lesson 5 **Semicolons and Colons** *Application*

A. Proofreading a Movie Review

The reporter who wrote this review of a science fiction movie was careless. She omitted semicolons and colons. Prepare her review for publishing by adding the needed semicolons and colons. Then rewrite the article correctly.

> Throughout this long, long movie, one thought kept popping into my mind I had seen this film before. But that was impossible it just opened at the Royal Theater yesterday. Even so, if you go to the movie, you may feel the same. It had the following common sci-fi films features never-ending special effects, a silly plot, and a weird setting. The movie began at 710 and ended at 905 I could have sworn I sat in that seat for at least six hours. The actors in this movie tried hard they just didn't have much to work with. I give this movie two ratings only one star for originality but three stars for special effects.

_____

_____

_____

_____

_____

_____

_____

_____

B. Writing Sentences with Semicolons and Colons

For each item, write a sentence that matches the description in parentheses.

EXAMPLE (sentence that uses a semicolon to join the parts of a compound sentence without a coordinating conjunction)
H. G. Wells was a scientist; he taught science in school and wrote a biology textbook.

1. (sentence that uses a colon in an expression of time)

_____

2. (sentence that uses a semicolon to join the parts of a compound sentence without a coordinating conjunction)

_____

3. (sentence that uses a colon to introduce a list of items)

_____

Copyright © McDougal Littell/Houghton Mifflin Company.

Hyphens, Dashes, and Parentheses

Teaching

Lesson 6

Here are ways to use the hyphen, the dash, and parentheses.

Hyphens Use a hyphen if part of a word must be carried over from one line to the next. Only words of two syllables or more may be broken, and each syllable must have at least two letters. Make sure that the word is separated between syllables.

Correct:	lad - der	be - tween	be - low
Incorrect:	ladd - er	bet - ween	bel - ow

Use hyphens in certain compound words, such as *self-made* and *great-uncle*.

Use hyphens in compound numbers from twenty-one through ninety-nine.

Use hyphens in spelled-out fractions, such as *one-third* and *four-fifths*.

Dashes Use dashes to show an abrupt break in thought.

The Big Dipper—if I can find it—is in the northern sky.

Parentheses Use parentheses to set off material that is loosely related to the rest of the sentence.

Orion (a hunter in Greek mythology) is also the name of a famous constellation.

A. Using Hyphens in Compound Words and Fractions

Write each of these words and phrases correctly, adding hyphens where needed.

1. sixty five moons _____

2. multiple star system _____

3. two thirds _____

4. light year _____

5. eighty eight constellations _____

B. Using Hyphens in Words Broken Between Lines

Underline each word that is broken correctly for use at the end of a line.

1. su-n, come-t, pl-anet, so-lar, Ve-nus, luna-r

2. J-upiter, plas-ma, Ma-rs, orbi-t, Sat-urn, u-niverse

C. Using Dashes and Parentheses

Add dashes and parentheses where they are needed in these sentences.

1. Light travels at the rate of 300,000 kilometers per second 186,000 miles per second.

2. Copernicus as you might know decided that the earth travels around the sun.

3. Halley's comet I've never seen it approaches the earth about every 76 years.

4. The world's largest telescope the Keck Telescope sits on a volcano in Hawaii.

5. The mass of one black hole my goodness! is estimated to be around 3.5 billion times that of the sun.

Copyright © McDougal Littell/Houghton Mifflin Company.

Copyright © McDougal Littell/Houghton Mifflin Company.

CHAPTER 9

Lesson 6

Hyphens, Dashes, and Parentheses

More Practice

A. Using Hyphens in Compound Words and Fractions

Write each of these words and phrases correctly, adding hyphens where needed.

1. forty four satellites _____

2. three quarters the size of the earth _____

3. sun like star _____

4. seventy seven telescopes _____

5. long lived stars _____

B. Using the Dash and Parentheses

Add dashes and parentheses where they are needed in these sentences.

1. Something I think is exciting you may think so too is seeing a shooting star.
2. The last meteor shower the one two nights ago was spectacular.
3. The truth is and you probably agree astronomers have much to learn about our universe.
4. Stars begin life as a cool mass in a nebula a cloud of gas and dust.
5. As he sets up the telescope, the astronomer hopes for a good night one with clear skies.

C. Using Hyphens, Dashes, and Parentheses Correctly

Rewrite each sentence, correcting punctuation errors. If a word at the end of a line is broken incorrectly, but there is a correct way of breaking it, show the word broken correctly in your revision. If the word may not be broken, move the entire word to the second line.

1. Astronomers estimate that the numbe- r of stars visible to the naked eye from Earth is around 8,000.

_____

_____

_____

2. Four thousand stars are visible from the northern hemisphere and—as you might guess 4,000 are visible fro- m the southern hemisphere.

_____

_____

_____

_____

3. At any one time, only 2,000 (of the 4,000 stars are visible from e- ither hemisphere.

_____

_____

_____

Hyphens, Dashes, and Parentheses

Application

A. Proofreading for Correct Punctuation

Rewrite this paragraph on the lines below, adding or correcting the placement of hyphens, dashes, and parentheses as needed.

> The sun is the most well known star at least among us Earthlings. Our sun is about 150,000,000 km (93,000,000 miles from the earth. However, the next closest star to our solar system is the triple—star Proxima Centauri. It is can you believe it? about 49 trillion km 25 trillion miles from Earth. In terms of the speed of light the standard used by astronomers to measure distance this triple—star is 4.29 light years distant. Light from the star takes as you might guess 4.29 years to reach Earth.

_____

_____

_____

_____

_____

_____

_____

B. Writing with Correct Punctuation

Follow the directions to write and punctuate sentences correctly.

1. Write a sentence containing a word that requires a hyphen.

_____

_____

2. Write a sentence that requires dashes and contains at least one word that needs a hyphen.

_____

_____

3. Write a sentence that requires parentheses and contains a word that needs a hyphen.

_____

_____

4. Write a sentence that requires dashes and contains a word that needs a hyphen.

_____

_____

Copyright © McDougal Littell/Houghton Mifflin Company.

CHAPTER 9

Lesson 6

CHAPTER 9

Lesson 7 Apostrophes

Teaching

Apostrophes in possessives Use an apostrophe to form the possessive of any noun, whether singular or plural. For a singular noun, add 's even if the word ends in s.

> Vondra's backpack   James's flashlight

For plural nouns that end in s, add only an apostrophe.

> the campers' sleeping bags   the rangers' warnings

For plural nouns that do not end in s, add an apostrophe and s.

> the deer's antlers   the men's boots

Apostrophes in contractions Use apostrophes in contractions to show where letters have been left out.

> I am --> I'm   we are --> we're   they have --> they've   she will --> she'll

Don't confuse contractions with possessive pronouns, which do not contain apostrophes.

> it's (contraction, means *it is*)   its (possessive, means *belonging to it*)

Apostrophes in plurals Use an apostrophe plus s to form the plurals of letters and words referred to as words.

> Remember to cross the ***t's*** and dot the ***i's*** on your signs.
> This sign has two ***and's*** in a row.

Using Apostrophes

In the sentences below, underline the correct word in the each pair in parentheses.

1. We found the (hikers/hikers') lost gear.
2. (It's/Its) a hard trek up the mountain.
3. This (parks/park's) rules were hard to understand.
4. The (rangers'/rangers) instructions helped.
5. (Weve/We've) got our backpacks and maps.
6. Did you see the (childrens'/children's) artwork?
7. You (shouldn't, should'nt) do (they're/their) homework for them.
8. He spells easy words wrong, for example, all his (*and's*/*ands*) and (*buts*/*but's*).
9. I asked (whose/who's) going to the school dance.
10. That climbing equipment is (Thomas'/Thomas's).
11. If Winona hears we're going, (shell/she'll) want to go along.
12. That shelf is for (women's/womens) shoes and boots.
13. That (fisherman's/fishermans') warnings probably saved our lives.
14. If (youve/you've) been here before, (you're, your) in for a surprise because of the changes.
15. When (you're, your) in the park, mind your (*p's*/*ps*) and (*qs*/*q's*).

Copyright © McDougal Littell/Houghton Mifflin Company.

Lesson 7 # Apostrophes

More Practice

A. Using Apostrophes Correctly

In each sentence below, underline the word that uses the apostrophe incorrectly or should have an apostrophe but does not. Then write the word correctly on the line.

1. The school has it's rules that we all have to follow. _____

2. He asked where the mens room is. _____

3. The teacher wanted us to print; he said our cursive *g*'s look like *qs*. _____

4. Jonathans excuse was that the dog ate it. _____

5. The womens' club meets every Monday. _____

6. Three boy's left their books in their lockers. _____

7. The authors corrections were not always legible. _____

8. I wonder what theyre going to bring. _____

9. Its a wonder you got any of those problems right. _____

10. Shes the one who can play difficult piano music. _____

B. Using Apostrophes in Possessives

Rewrite this paragraph on the lines below, replacing all underlined phrases with phrases using possessives with apostrophes.

     The national parks are <u>the heritage of the nation</u>. This fact suggests how we should use them. The parks represent <u>the natural history of our country</u> and are impossible to replace if damaged. Think of the Grand Canyon, of <u>the geysers of Yosemite</u>, and of <u>the giant trees of Sequoia</u>. Think, too, of <u>the giant volcanic crater of Haleakala</u> on the island of Maui. These natural wonders existed in <u>the world of our ancestors</u>. Let us preserve them intact for <u>the delight of our children</u>.

_____

_____

_____

_____

_____

_____

_____

Copyright © McDougal Littell/Houghton Mifflin Company.

CHAPTER 9

Lesson 7

Apostrophes   *Application*

A. Proofreading for Use of the Apostrophe

Proofread the paragraph below for errors in the use of apostrophes. If a word uses an apostrophe incorrectly or is lacking a needed apostrophe, cross out the word. Then draw a caret ⌃ next to the error and write the word correctly above the error.

> If youve ever visited one of our national parks, your familiar with the park rangers. The rangers' main jobs are to protect the parks and to help visitor's enjoy them. Each ranger's duties are varied. A ranger whose leading a nature hike needs to know about the animals in the area. Hikers might ask about different animal's tracks or a birds call. If history is important at they're park, rangers should be able to answer visitors' questions about whats happened there. Theyll have to explain things clearly and politely. Whenever Ive been in a park, theyve been extremely helpful.

B. Using Apostrophes in Writing

First rewrite each phrase listed below, using a possessive with an apostrophe. Then use the phrases that you created in a paragraph about an incident on a camping excursion.

the late arrival of the campers _____

the inexperience of the guide _____

the food supplies of the camp _____

the cleverness of the raccoons _____

_____

_____

_____

_____

_____

_____

_____

_____

_____

_____

Copyright © McDougal Littell/Houghton Mifflin Company.

Lesson 8

Punctuating Titles

Teaching

Quotation marks, italics, and underlining used correctly in titles show what kind of work or selection is named.

Quotation marks Use quotation marks to set off the titles of short works.

Quotation Marks for Titles			
Book chapter	"Summer Days," from *Charlotte's Web*	**Magazine article**	"Hands and Hearts"
Short story	"Scout's Honor"	**Song**	"Streets of Laredo"
Essay	"Americans All"	**Poem**	"Analysis of Baseball"

Italics and underlining Use italics for titles of longer works and for the names of ships, trains, spacecraft, and individual airplanes (not the type of plane). In handwriting, use underlining to indicate words that should be in italics in printed material.

Italics or Underlines for Titles			
Book	*Stuart Little*	**Epic poem**	*The Odyssey*
Play	*The Miricle Worker*	**Painting**	*American Gothic*
Magazine	*Time*	**Ship**	U.S.S. *Arizona*
Movie	*James and the Giant Peach*	**Train**	*Twentieth-Century Limited*
Long musical selection or CD	*Peter and the Wolf*	**Airplane or Spacecraft**	*Columbia*

Punctuating Titles Correctly

Write each sentence, using quotation marks or underlining correctly to set off titles.

1. In the Louvre Museum, in Paris, you can see the Mona Lisa.

_____

2. Ann did her book report on Ben and Me; her favorite chapter was The Lightning Rod.

_____

3. The Ransom of Red Chief is a funny short story by O. Henry.

_____

4. In Baltimore harbor, we photographed the U.S.S. Constellation.

_____

5. The Dance of the Sugarplum Fairy is a melody in The Nutcracker Suite.

_____

6. My father once rode the New York Central Railroad's famous Empire State train.

_____

Copyright © McDougal Littell/Houghton Mifflin Company.

CHAPTER 9

Punctuating Titles

More Practice

A. Punctuating Titles Correctly

In each sentence below, insert quotation marks where needed and underline words that should be italicized.

1. William Shakespeare wrote Hamlet, King Lear, Macbeth, and Romeo and Juliet.

2. For homework, we have to read two chapters of Johnny Tremaine.

3. The artist's title for "Whistler's Mother" was Study in Gray and Black.

4. Two poems by Robert Frost are The Road Not Taken and Mending Wall.

5. The U.S.S. Constitution is also known as "Old Ironsides."

6. I get the Titanic confused with the Lusitania.

7. Naomi's favorite song from the musical My Fair Lady is On the Street Where You Live.

8. We saw a production of Oklahoma! by a touring company.

9. The magazine Calliope is all about world history.

10. The President of the United States flies on Air Force One.

B. Punctuating Titles Correctly

Use each title given in parentheses in a sentence, punctuating the title correctly.

1. (patriotic song: Yankee Doodle) _____

_____

2. (long musical work by Ludwig van Beethoven: Fifth Symphony) _____

_____

3. (short story featuring Sherlock Holmes: The Speckled Band) _____

_____

4. (poem from *Alice in Wonderland:* Jabberwocky) _____

_____

5. (lunar landing craft: The Eagle) _____

_____

Copyright © McDougal Littell/Houghton Mifflin Company.

Lesson 8 · Punctuating Titles

Application

Punctuating Titles Correctly

Several titles of literary or musical works are listed below. Add underlining or quotation marks to the listed titles. Then write a paragraph that includes at least five of the titles. Include other works that are not listed, if you wish. Be sure to punctuate correctly. (Suggestion: In your paragraph, explain to a friend why you like or dislike—or think you would like or dislike—some of the works listed.)

Books

The Indian in the Cupboard

Charlotte's Web

Holes

The Westing Game

Poems

The Tyger

The Walrus and the Carpenter

Light in the Attic

The Owl and the Pussycat

Short Stories

Rip Van Winkle

The Little Match Girl

Dr. Jekyll and Mr. Hyde

The Happy Prince

Plays

Oklahoma!

Hamlet

The Sound of Music

Romeo and Juliet

_____

_____

_____

_____

_____

_____

_____

_____

_____

_____

Copyright © McDougal Littell/Houghton Mifflin Company.

Sentence Parts

Complete each diagram with the sentence provided.

A. Simple Subjects and Verbs

Shirley sings.

We will be listening.

B. Compound Subjects and Verbs

Compound Subject Shirley and Michael sing.

Compound Verb Shirley sings and dances.

Compound Subject and Verb Singers and dancers rehearse and perform.

Copyright © McDougal Littell/Houghton Mifflin Company.

Sentence Parts

Complete each diagram with the sentence provided.

C. Adjectives and Adverbs

My best friend often sings very loudly.

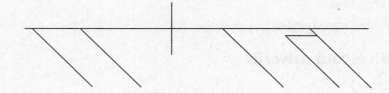

Shirley and my best friend sometimes harmonize.

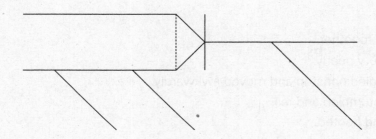

Do you sing fairly decently?

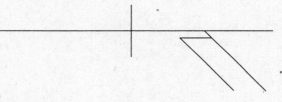

Sing along!

The singers' friends and relatives come and listen.

Copyright © McDougal Littell/Houghton Mifflin Company.

DIAGRAMMING

Sentence Parts

Application

On a separate piece of paper, diagram each of these sentences.

A. Diagramming Simple and Compound Subjects and Verbs

1. Classmates were performing.
2. Performers and crew had prepared.
3. Mothers and fathers applauded and cheered.

B. Diagramming Adjectives and Adverbs

1. Michael dances very skillfully.
2. Does that able dancer sing well, too?
3. Dance students watched carefully.

C. Mixed Practice

1. Shirley and Michael danced together.
2. They intentionally danced very poorly.
3. The usually graceful girl giggled nonstop and moved awkwardly.
4. Suddenly clumsy, Michael stumbled and fell.
5. My friends and I laughed and hooted.
6. We and the comic performers grinned and left reluctantly..

Copyright © McDougal Littell/Houghton Mifflin Company.

Complements

Complete each diagram with the sentence provided.

A. Subject Complements

Predicate Noun Nelson is Enrique's closest friend.

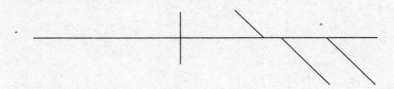

The two boys are neighbors and classmates.

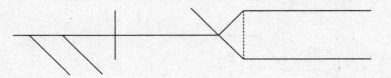

Predicate Adjective One boy is quite shy.

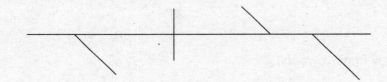

His friend is much more friendly and outgoing.

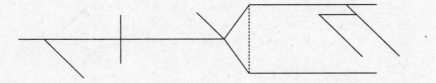

Copyright © McDougal Littell/Houghton Mifflin Company.

Name _____ Date _____

Complements

right>*More Practice 2*

Complete each diagram with the sentence provided.

B. Direct Objects

Single Direct Object Nelson's family left Cuba recently.

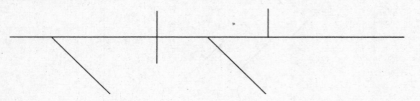

Compound Direct Object He is still learning English words and American customs.

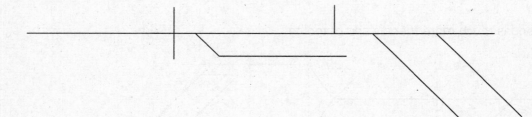

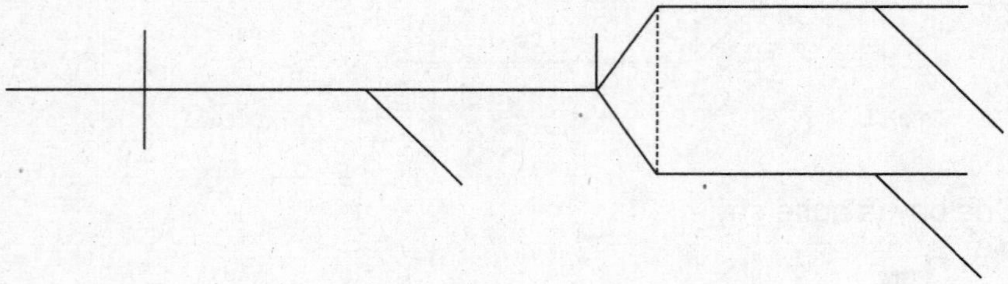

C. Indirect Objects

Enrique is teaching Nelson many English words.

Nelson and his family teach Enrique their customs and stories.

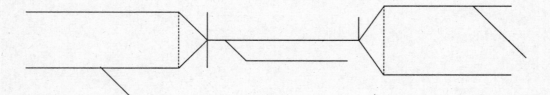

188 GRAMMAR FOR WRITING WORKBOOK

Copyright © McDougal Littell/Houghton Mifflin Company.

Complements

Application

On a separate piece of paper, diagram each of these sentences.

A. Diagramming Subject Complements

1. A new country can be very difficult.
2. Are you an immigrant, too?
3. Enrique is a good teacher.

B. Diagramming Direct and Indirect Objects

1. Enrique speaks English and Spanish.
2. Nelson's other classmates and his teacher give him special help, too.
3. The experience is bringing everyone benefits.

C. Mixed Practice

1. Many Americans are immigrants or immigrants' children.
2. The English language gives most newcomers some problems.
3. English is a difficult language.
4. Maybe you were lucky.
5. Maybe your parents taught you English immediately.
6. Babies learn words and language rules easily.

Copyright © McDougal Littell/Houghton Mifflin Company.

Prepositional Phrases

Complete each diagram with the sentence provided.

Adjective Prepositional Phrases

Sixth-graders at Marnie's school are excited.

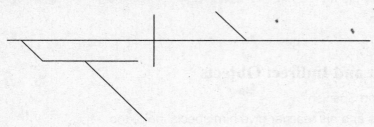

Marnie and members of her class are planning a field trip to Washington, D.C.

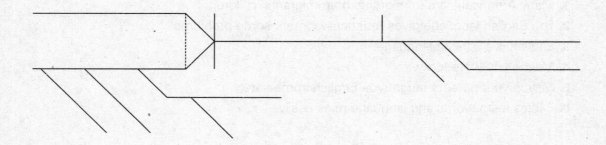

The cost of rooms for the students and their chaperones will be high.

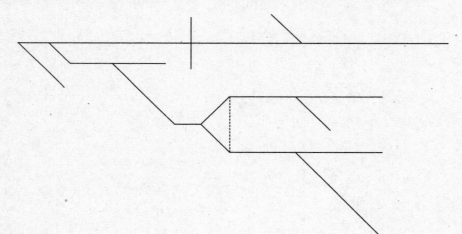

Copyright © McDougal Littell/Houghton Mifflin Company.

Prepositional Phrases

More Practice 2

Complete each diagram with the sentence provided.

Adverb Prepositional Phrases

A class meeting was held in the gym.

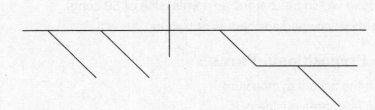

At that time, the class president described several ideas to the class.

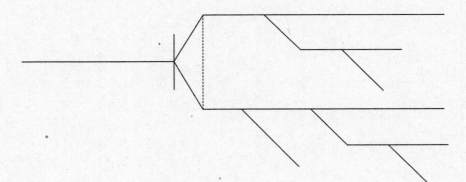

Committees are looking into the ideas and will report back to the class.

Copyright © McDougal Littell/Houghton Mifflin Company.

Prepositional Phrases

Application

On a separate piece of paper, diagram each of these sentences.

A. Diagramming Adjective Prepositional Phrases

1. One group of sixth-graders developed a design for a fun house.
2. Each customer at the fun house would be charged an admisssion of 50 cents.
3. Students in favor of a talent show planned a schedule of tryouts.

B. Diagramming Adverb Prepositional Phrases

1. The fun house will be built in the school gymnasium.
2. Plans called for contributions from area businesses.
3. At the second class meeting, class members and their teachers discussed decorations.

C. Mixed Practice

1. The cost of the fun house made it impractical.
2. A majority of the class wanted a talent show.
3. During the discussion, enthusiasm for the project grew rapidly.
4. Students split into little groups and talked eagerly.
5. Marnie was one of the fashion-conscious girls.
6. They liked the idea of a funny fashion show.

Copyright © McDougal Littell/Houghton Mifflin Company.

DIAGRAMMING

Compound Sentences

Complete each diagram with the sentence provided.

The class president called for a vote, and the students adopted a talent show for their fundraiser.

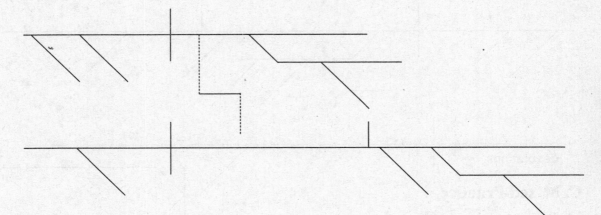

Two people became the show coordinators, and they gave the principal a report on their plans.

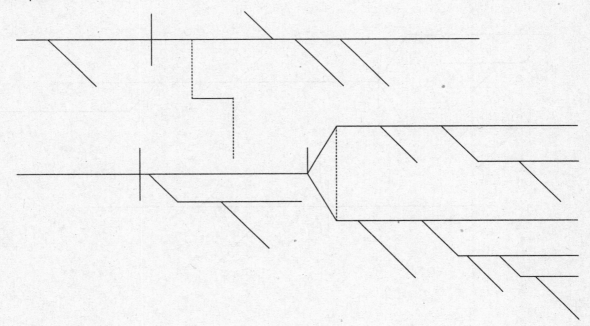

Copyright © McDougal Littell/Houghton Mifflin Company.

Compound Sentences

Complete each diagram with the sentence provided.

Marnie's classmates were always in committee meetings, or they were collecting materials for costumes and props.

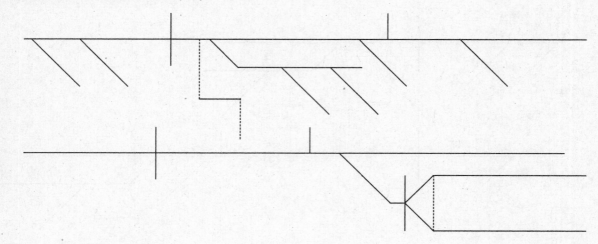

Rehearsals and other preparations were a lot of work, but they were fun, too.

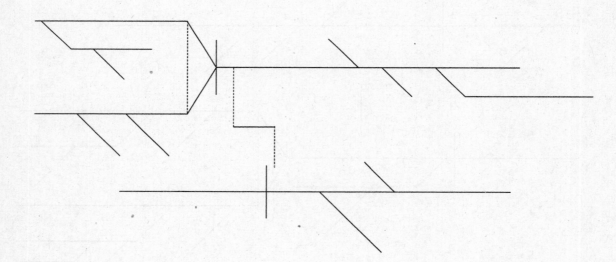

Copyright © McDougal Littell/Houghton Mifflin Company.

Compound Sentences

On a separate piece of paper, diagram each of these sentences.

Diagramming Compound Sentences

1. The jurors watched all of the tryouts, and then they chose the best ones.
2. Students sang or danced, or they performed skits.
3. Some students did not get a spot in the program, but they worked backstage.
4. A publicity committee sent the newspaper information about the show, and students sold ads in the program.
5. Some parents helped in the preparations, but the students did most of the work.
6. Finally, the night of the talent show arrived, and a big crowd gave the performers loud applause.

Copyright © McDougal Littell/Houghton Mifflin Company.